N by E

ROCKWELL KENT

NEW YORK LITERARY GUILD 1930

To

FRANCES!

PREFACE

IN THIS BOOK *is told the story of an actual voyage to Greenland in a small boat; of shipwreck there and of what, if anything, happened afterwards. Yet it may not be called the story of that adventure but rather one story of at least three different ones that three quite different men might write. It is my tale. And if an author in recording what has interested himself differs from editors—so everlastingly concerned with what may interest others, he may no less, knowing himself the only worthwhile thing for him to be,* hope *that a*

ix

hundred thousand souls will see him as the mirror of them-
selves—and buy his book.

There are many books on Greenland—on the country, its
history, its government, its people; but above all of them are
the stories told by the Greenlanders themselves. And these
have been written down by Knud Rasmussen.

The story of "The Sealer from Aluk whose Heart Burst
when he Saw the Sun Rising above his Dwelling-place,"
to which I give a chapter of this book, is found, in English, in
the work, "Greenland," *published by the Commission for*
the Direction of the Geological and Geographic Investiga-
tions in Greenland. The story about "The Woman who
was so Beautiful that wherever she was the Sea was Calm"
I have translated, freely, from the German of a Rasmussen
book called "Grönlandsagen" *published by Gyldendahl.*

Rather than name, here at the beginning of this book,
those many Danes for whose hospitality in Greenland and
Denmark I am so grateful, I have chosen to invite them all
to the Christening party of the next to last chapter, where,
released to utterance by the festivities of the occasion, I could
more eloquently thank them.   R. K.

Ausable Forks, N. Y.
    August, 1930

THE FULL PAGE "ILLUSTRATIONS"

of this volume are less illustrative of the text than supplementary to it. They are reproduced from wood block prints and bear the following titles:

Hail and Farewell, The Bowsprit, The Lookout, and Night Watch are here published by courtesy of The A. C. F. Company

I

« AND my son,» said Arthur Allen drawing back his shoulders, tilting on his heels, clasping his hands to the blaze behind him, looking beyond me as if he were smiling at God—«and my son—is going to sail to Greenland in a small boat.»

«God! May I go with him?»

«You may—if he is willing.»

SAM ALLEN came to my house. He was a beauty! Tall—over six feet, strong and lithe; slow moving, slow and courteous of speech, and calm. And if his calmness was phlegmatic it nevertheless lent his presence that dignity which is essential to commanders. Here was the captain—and a good one. He was an experienced sailor; and he had that serene self-confidence which happenings can bring to some men. He loved the sea and he was made for it. Sam Allen and the sea, two elements; they could well contemplate each other, endlessly; and neither ever know what other signified.

* 4 *

THERE was a certain man who lived in the suburbs of New York. And every week-day morning, for years, he took the 7:45 train to the great city; and every day on the 5:15 came home. He owned, we guess, a little house. It had a furnace to be his winter care and a front lawn for summer. He had a radio set and a motor car, and a wife. One night they would play bridge, another they would go to the movies; and on Sunday afternoon they would go motoring. It seemed as if things would go on and on like this, always; until at last he would die. And that would have been his life.

Now there are certain islands in the South Seas so far away that everyone believes them to be paradise. Summer is eternal there. And in the cool shadows of their groves recline fair youths and maidens happy in being and through happiness forever young.

When the vision of these islands broke upon the commuter suddenly the little round of his activities became unendurable. His imagination took fire and in the aura of the conflagration he saw himself sailing the broad Pacific, landing, a sunburned mariner, on those flowering coral shores. He closed his eyes; the newspaper fell from his hands. Love, love enveloped him; soft hands and lips caressed him; the air was laden with sweet perfume and the song of birds. Oh Paradise!

So he must build a boat; about them he knew nothing. He began to study. With unwearying purpose he gave himself to the reading of every authority on boat design, he filled himself with lore and facts. He studied catalogues, he looked at craft. And he came to know them. He came to know, moreover, what he wanted. It must be a small boat and a staunch boat; roomy and broad of beam. It must be a safe boat, seaworthy and able. And he drew a plan.

Her keel was laid in a little ship-yard on the Hudson; and from that day to the day of the boat's completion her designer watched her growth as only a man about to sail the seven seas for Paradise would watch his magic craft evolve. He combed the lumber yards for the soundest planks and timbers that the forests yielded. He followed them through the hands of the carpenters, saw the timbers cut and joined and bolted into place. No little detail could escape his scrutiny, no defect elude him.

And what it cost! And how he could have justified that cost at home! What could he say that would conceal the truth of his exalted plans?

And so in the growing excitement of the enterprise the years flew by; the boat was nearly done. What hope must then have beamed in the commuter's countenance, what intimation of approaching glory! If these signs sought concealment through a special tenderness at home, that tenderness was their betrayal. Was not the boat itself an unfoldment of his own spirit, an opening of the book of his own dreams, the materializing in such symbol as the world might understand of his most secret self? Just as all men must some day put off the drab clothes of this world to put on the shining raiment of immortality, and in that moment for a moment stand in nakedness revealed before their Maker, so at almost the very moment that this poor man was to step into his swan boat, his wife, we only guess, confronted him.

«What,»—arms akimbo—«do you think you're going to do in that boat?»

«I was going,» he answered with quiet determination, «to sail to Par—to the South Seas.»

«You're not.»

And there, true or not, ends one of the saddest stories in the world.

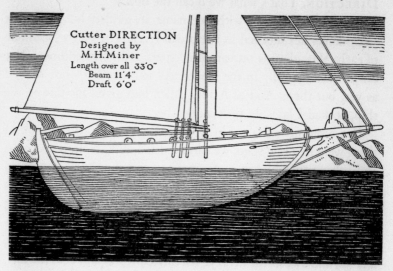

Cutter DIRECTION
Designed by
M. H. Miner
Length over all 33′0″
Beam 11′4″
Draft 6′0″

THE boat lay nearly built when Arthur Allen bought her; he took her finishing in hand. All that was good he bettered—and the best he doubled. And when the three ton iron shoe was bolted to her oaken keel we thought God help the rocks she hits! Then she was launched and named.

There was to me something forbidding about her name, ominous I could not then have said; however, subsequent events incline me now to read such meaning into it. The name, a proclamation of man's will, was an encroachment on the special and sole virtue of the Gods. *Seem* to be carefree, light of heart and gay—the very elements will love you. Call your ship Daisy or Bouncing Bess—and the sun of life will sparkle on that course where fair winds drive her laughingly along. «There is,» said

* 8 *

Arthur Allen, «one most essential thing a man must have in life, DIRECTION. That's what we'll call the boat.»

And now *Direction* with her name in golden letters on her stern flanks lies moored in the broad river. The bright sunshine of early May glistens on varnished spars and polished brass. Her tawny sails flap idly in the breeze. All is on board—not stowed as yet, but there. And as Arthur Allen had given his care to the ship, so had I lavishly provisioned her.

For economy of space in stowing the provisions the bulk of them were in a raw state; we carried dried milk, fruit, beans, peas and other vegetables in preference to canned articles, though of these we had a small supply for use in such rough weather as might prohibit cooking. Of eggs we had twenty-four dozen, gathered fresh-laid from the countryside and preserved in water-glass. Potatoes, onions and cabbages we had in quantity; oranges, a crate; and sweets for luxury. We carried wood and coal for fuel, and kerosene for light; tobacco and cigarettes—no, these arrived too late. We loaded them in Nova Scotia.

So now for Nova Scotia the *Direction* sails. There we're to join her, Skipper Sam and I; there we're to recondition her, from there set sail. And yet this first departure was for Arthur Allen an event, a touching one. Few men in all their lives are moved to give so much to any enterprise as he had given here. The boat at last was his achievement—for his son. And it was above all in tribute to himself that Arthur Allen's friends stood around him there that day to see his boat depart.

The mate and two men are in charge. They cast off. The water widens in their wake. The mate goes below.

«Goodbye, goodbye!» cries everyone.

* 9 *

Suddenly the mate pops up again. «Say,» he bawls, «where in hell are those cigarettes?»

OUR crew, as Captain Sam at last made it, was to consist of three: him, me and one called Cupid. Cupid was in Paris. «Oh, well,» he wrote his friend, «I'll go with you this once.» And he bestirred himself at last and came. He was a big fellow, huge. His vast muscles were encased in fat. He had curly golden hair, a face like his name, and the expression of a petulant potato. He was an experienced and competent sailor. He would discourse on navigation with a familiarity that was disconcerting, and so bewildering a technical vocabulary that, amateur navigator as I had presumed to be, I could only stammer my incomprehension. And I was brought to wonder then why Sam, who knew his friend's accomplishments so well, had chosen me to be his navigator. Cupid, as the mate, proved grand; humanly he was offensive; while financially he was a disappointment and, at last, a liability.

We have left *Direction* following, at Cupid's whim, her nose to Nova Scotia. First she stuck it into a barge in the passage of Hell Gate and broke it; then she nosed into Westport for a few days' jamboree, into Provincetown for local color and to whine again for cigarettes, into Halifax that the mate might gild the lily of his navigation under the guidance of a local master; and at last, two days before us, she arrived in the Bradore lakes and anchored at Baddeck.

There for a week we worked. *Direction* was hauled out, repaired and scraped and painted. The skipper worked on the hull and rigging; I made shelves and racks for stores, and stowed provisions; my fair wife scrubbed and polished; and the mate heavily betook himself from one berth to the other, at request, and smoked. Inertness can infuriate as nothing else; not only were we daily confronted and hampered by that heavy presence, but the very disorder and dirt and the filthy utensils that we contended with were themselves the accumulation of a full month's slothfulness. Of slothfulness the ravaged stores were evidence: half of the eggs had been consumed and most of the canned goods; while perishable supplies had been left soaking in the water of the bilge.

The skipper showed himself temperamentally disinclined to meddle with ship's discipline even when riot and mutiny were imminent. They were. Here at the outset of an enterprise on which three men must live for weeks in the confinement of a little boat, to be day in and out each other's world of human kind, one man had proved so gross a shirker of responsibility and work as to endanger the morale of the expedition. If we could only sail, I thought, things may be different; and with the thought of removing at once the thorn that festered in my disposition and the mountain that obstructed our movements, I demanded that while I was on the boat the mate should stay off. Off he stayed. Now we could work!—and sing about it.

Clothes were washed and hung to dry. Bedding was aired. The soaked food was spread in the sun to dry, and packed again in tins, and stowed. We improved the conveniences of the main cabin and so remodeled the narrow dreary forecastle that was to be my quarters that only *Direction's* last convulsions could disturb the order of its shelves.

Too often is a boat's *inside* neglected although the value of living is conditional upon how. It is essential but hardly enough that a house roof be tight. We assume that, and proceed to the establishing of conveniences and comforts within, knowing well how closely they concern our happiness. Fundamentals are important—but they are merely what we build upon, and of themselves of little value. Of what use is it to build your house foundation on a rock if you don't build a house on the foundation; if you don't make a home of the house; lure a woman to the home, beget children and establish a line of archangels that will go on and on forever? What use in merely being safe at sea? Rear on that restless element your structure of non-fundamental all essential comfort so that you may at least occasionally *think* without a world of dishes, food and what-nots crashing on your head.

So, using the little time and the few tools and materials I had to the utmost, I did, during the hours of the mate's exclusion from the cabin, build myself so secure and comfortable a little retreat in the cramped forecastle of the boat that I could thereafter withdraw from his dull presence at every leisure moment, day and night, that came to me. And did.

AT FOUR-THIRTY in the afternoon of June 17th we sailed. The exasperating delay that had put off our sailing until that date, and on that date until that hour, the misgivings I had felt about the mate, all were forgotten in that moment of leave taking. The bright sun shone upon us; the lake was blue under the westerly breeze, and luminous, how luminous! the whole far world of our imagination. How like a colored lens the colored present! through it we see the forward vista of our lives. Here, in the measure that the water widened in our wake and heart strings stretched to almost breaking, the golden future neared us and enfolded us, made us at last—how soon!—oblivious to all things but the glamour of adventure. And while one world diminished, narrowed and then disappeared, before us a new world unrolled and neared us to display itself. Who can deny the human soul its everlasting need to make the unknown known; not for the sake of knowing, not to inform itself or be informed or wise, but for the need to exercise the need to know? What is that need but the imagination's hunger for the new and raw materials of its creative trade? Of things and facts assured to us and known we've got to make the best, and live with it. That humdrum is the price of living. We *live* for those fantastic and unreal moments of beauty which our thoughts may build upon the passing panorama of experience.

Soon all that we had ever seen before was left behind and a new land of fields and farms, pastures and meadows, woods and open lands and rolling hills was streaming by, all in the mellow splendor of late afternoon in June, all green and clean and beautiful. We stripped and plunged ahead into the blue water; and catching hold of a rope as it swept by, trailed in the wake. It was so warm— the water and the early summer air. So we shall live all summer naked, and get brown and magnificent!

I cooked supper: hot baking-powder biscuit and—I don't remember what. «You're a wonderful cook!» said everyone. So I washed the dishes and put the cabin in order.

«Oh,» thought I, «people are nice! the world is grand! I'm happy! God is good!»

TWILIGHT, the ocean, eight o-clock have come; I take the helm on my watch. The wind has risen, the horizon is dark against a livid sky. It's cold. Never again for months to come do my thoughts run to nakedness. Nor do I see green fields, nor thriving homesteads, nor people long enough except to part from them; nor—though it's June—the summer; not for a thousand miles. And as it darkens and the stars come out, and the black sea appears unbroken everywhere save for the restless turbulence of its own plain, as the lights are extinguished in the cabin,—then I am suddenly alone. And almost terror grips me for I now *feel* the solitude; under the keel and overhead the depths,—and me, enveloped in immensity.

How strange to be here in a little boat!—and not by accident, not cast adrift here from a wreck, but purposely! What purpose, whose? And if I call to mind how I have read of Greenland and for years have longed to go there, how I have read and read again the Iceland sagas and been stirred by them, how I've been moved by the strange story of the Greenland settlements and their tragic end, by all the glamour and the mystery of those adventures, how I have followed in the wake of Leif and found America, and how by all of that I've come to need to know those countries, tread their soil, to touch the ancient stones of their enclosures, sail their seas to think myself a Viking like themselves, —then I may boast that *purpose* and *my* will have brought me here. And yet this very moment is the contradiction of it. The darkness and the wind! the imponderable immensity of space and elements! My frail hands grip the tiller; my eyes stare hypnotically at the stars beyond the tossing masthead or watch the bow wave as we part the seas. I hold the course. I have no thought or will, no power, to alter it.

So midnight comes; I rouse the captain. Chilled to the bone I go below, make coffee, wash up and turn in. Cold, but more tired, I sleep.

I CAME from my dim forecastle into a cabin illuminated by the morning sun. Beyond the open hatch, braced at the tiller, sat the mate, his yellow oilskins glistening under flying spray. Breakfast! «How about coffee?» and I reach out a cup to the mate.

«Just a moment,» says the mate in strangely muffled, hasty tones, and he leans suddenly over the side. «Good,» says he a moment later, wiping his mouth as he sits up again, «Now let's have the coffee.» And he drinks it up.

The mound of blankets in the captain's berth resolves itself into the captain; devours, still sleeping, a hearty breakfast; draws the blankets over itself again, and again is mound. Even so must do the dead into whose tombs their friends with loving care put food and wine. Even so may do we all and call it life—but I no way believe it. It is eight o'clock and I relieve the mate on watch. Whew! what a cold north wind and white capped sea! Dream? here is reality so real it nips the bone.

We're in the midst of a stampeding myriad of white-maned beasts of Neptune, rearing their crests and backs against the sky, rushing upon us to overwhelm us, tossing us. We ride them, we hold our course close hauled for Channel. The wind is rising and we ought to reef. At ten o'clock we shorten sail and are hove to under staysail. So we ride out the hours of my watch.

T IS five minutes before noon when the captain relieves me. I go below. With tremors that I will not show I carefully, bracing myself against the violent tossing of the boat, open a square varnished wooden case and, letting no fingers touch its silver arc, lift out my beautiful and precious sextant.

Inside, on the lid of the box, is secured a card; its heading reads:

THE NATIONAL PHYSICAL LABORATORY
CERTIFICATE OF EXAMINATION
CLASS A

and after various preliminary statements of fact about the instrument, including that «The shades and mirrors are good,» informs the reader that it has no error.

I have had this instrument for years and never used it. Never known how. Its mere possession moved me. Often I have opened its case and looked at it—so beautifully contrived and made, and its bright arc so cleanly and minutely graduated. And once I found that someone had laid hands on it, for there, oxidized upon the silver, was a great thumb print. But not even to cleanse it of that would I touch it, for a stain can less obscure the graduations of that arc than the erosion of polishing.

And now at last, at noon of the 18th of June in the year nineteen twenty-nine, having for nearly forty-seven years knocked about the world East, West, North and South, in high places and in low, and been more or less finger printed and soiled but— pray God!—not too much polished off, I propose to take my sextant in hand, cautiously creep along the pitching, tossing, rolling desk of my small ship, mount to the highest place against the mast, twist my legs around the halyards, brace my shoulders between them, and, resting one eye as it were on that fixed point of the absolute, the sun, and the other on the immutable horizon of this earth, find by triangulation where I am. And if, after combining with my calculations on that sectant reading every mitigating factor the equation calls for, I choose to publish the result in the cryptic terms of degrees and minutes, it may be understood that I am not too proud of where I found myself.

I was, we were, I figured it, in lat. 45° 55′ 20″ N. And for being about sixty miles wrong in my result I can only plead that I had never figured a sight before.

Now plain work-a-day navigation is not a difficult science. It can easily be mastered by a reasonably logical mind. And yet that reasonable logic is enough to bar anyone from acquiring the least glimmering of navigation from the average routine navigator. How many times have I not, with bridge privileges at sea, tried to learn something about his art from the second officer or captain. The most that I could get was such an arbitrary rule of thumb as could prove only exasperating to one who needed to know *why*. And when once without a rule or text-book I had of myself contrived a system so that a child might have comprehended it, a captain dismissed it because it was unorthodox and set me down as a hopeless sinner. And because captains are all like that, and all text-books have been made by captains, I might have finally despaired of myself—but that I knew a poet who happened to be a mate and, more than that, a Dane. And words were images to him, and stars were playthings of his thoughts. He taught me for a day. And all I know of navigation stems from there. All that I know is little. I can find my latitude and my longitude; I can cross them and know the spot I'm standing on. I can plot my great circle course and, allowing for the deviation and the error of my compass, lay it. And that's all. But I've seen men who, with all the systems of the universe at their finger-tips, knew less.

«Why don't you try your Sumner line, or Saint Hilaire's?» said I to the mate of the *Direction*.

«Why?» he answered and turned over.

ALL day the wind continued; the barometer was falling. At four o'clock we set a double reefed mainsail; we were getting nowhere. Below, in the cabin, the inadequacy of the standard equipment of racks and drawers was displaying itself in the growing confusion of the place. Nature and human nature were at odds; chaos versus order, wind and water, gravity and centrifugal force versus the frail fabric of the human disposition. And against such odds we had not merely to contain ourselves but to create, build up, more flesh and blood and bone and nerves against the ravages of the moment and the erosion of passing time. We hungered and we ate. And if ever I am challenged at the bar of heaven to account for my stewardship on earth I'll say: «Remember, Lord, that when you

* 24 *

most harassed me, when you set pandemonium loose on my appointed task, when you put out my fires, suffocated me with smoke, poured red hot coals upon my feet, upset my kettles scalding me with boiling soup; when, not content with this, you kicked and struck me, knocked me down and rubbed my nose in all of it—there, then and always without fail, on time—I served hot meals, and good ones.»

And, if there is heavenly justice, and if the mate by any chance passes the outer police courts of eternity, judgment will read: «You ate the eggs and canned goods on Long Island Sound.»

IF ANYTHING, the wind and sea increased that night. Motionless in the narrow cockpit, drenched by the flying spray of icy seas, chilled by the wind, four hours seemed eternity. A liner passed us to the westward bound for Sydney, a slowly pitching carnival of light; passed and was lost again over the black rim of the world. How dark it is!

A low light is burning in the cabin; and in the binnacle a feeble lamp. Squalls strike us; the lamp flickers and goes almost out. There are no stars. You watch the compass card; and all the rest of the universe is sound and feeling. Feeling of wind and wet and cold, feeling of lifting seas and steep descents, of rolling over as the wind gusts hit; and sound?—of wind in the shrouds, of hard spray flung on drum-tight canvas, of rushing water at the scuppers, of the gale shearing a tormented sea.

* 26 *

Midnight; the skipper takes the deck. The stove is out. It's a cold forecastle and damp that is my room, and water has leaked through the hatch into my blankets; all nothing to a tired man. My blankets are of magic stuff; drawing them over me I'm wrapped in sleep.

Soon after midnight the light at Cape Ray was sighted. The headwind had already put us miles to the eastward of our course to clear the cape, and in the hours elapsing till we neared the land we made more leeway. The choice was then of making port or of coming about on a long westward tack to sea. The wind by now amounted to a gale.

Youth's judgment sets the stage for its own courage; we kept at sea. And when I took my watch at eight, there, astern and off our starboard beam, lay Newfoundland.

Not Newfoundland as I had first seen it here at sunrise years ago, a brown and golden land with the sun glistening from its mountain faces and from the spires of Channel, but a grim land shrouded in scud, steel gray against the low dark ceiling of the sky. No threatening sky; it made its promise good. The norther raged, lashing the mountain seas, beating their crests and whipping them to vapor. And every hour increased its fury. Slow work and hard to beat to windward in a gale like this! Slow work and useless as the outcome proved.

There was no comfort on board and nobody cared. On duty you hung to the tiller and took what came. Off duty you went to bed. Water dripped through on everything and when the boat rolled over bilge water flooded the shelves above the cabin berths. And roll she did! Roll till her running lights rolled under; sailed with them there. And you hung on and wondered—

wondered—if she'd right herself again. And pitch! How she would lift and ride those short, steep seas! climb to their tops till, over-balanced there, she'd pitch head foremost to the trough with the resounding smash of her broad cheeks and thirteen tons on water. And from my forecastle I thought: «The keel is an iron casting weighing three tons. It is secured to the boat by vertical iron bolts. On the end of these are nuts screwed upon slender threads. It is these threads that hold that iron to the boat. God, is that all!»

Long before noon, having put Cape Ray so far to the east-ward of us that there appeared some hope that we could weather it, we came about; and by the hours that followed proved that in such wind and sea *Direction*, with every brave appearance of sailing a northerly course, could go exactly east and west; no more. And so much for a name.

But the ocean is of three dimensions; and if we could negotiate but one of them the wonder is that we were spared the third. Stripped to a double-reefed mainsail, *Direction* fought; she took her beating and her knock-downs and came back for more; and, as that evening we tacked into the little port of Channel, the low sun broke through the clouds to greet us and display us clothed in glory to the wondering crowd.

OH NEWFOUNDLAND! How young I was when I first came to you, and how at this revisitation the memory of my illusions rises to reproach me! Here, I believed, in this remote, uncultivated land must live a people kind through necessity, wise in unworldly ways, strong, virile, brave and good by grace of God. And the very day lent an appropriate beauty to that country as I saw it first. It was early morning, cloudless and immaculately clear. Far away over the dark blue plain of the ocean stood the land. It gleamed and sparkled in the sunshine and its high mountains topped with new fallen snow appeared as emblems of that moral loveliness with which my ardent thoughts had vested it. Oh, how I see it now in memory, that Paradise!

And it appeared, when I had come to land and traveled there, that every heart in every village of the countryside was gay, for it was fall; and men, months absent at the fisheries, had now come home. Men stored their crops and nets, made tight their homes; and brides and wives laid beds for the long winter nights of love. No wonder that I came to live there!

This, in that drama of disillusionment, let us call «scene I,» and pass with my memory to the drama's end; last act, last scene. St. Johns, the harbor front. The city, grimy and picturesque, its soot pall hanging in the August air. Crowds on the wharf waving Farewell-God-bless-yous toward the New York liner's rail; but not at me who stand there quite alone but for, beside me, a little stocky man with a great Nick Carter black mustache, a cigar in his mouth and a Derby on one side of his head.

«So you've come down to see me off?» say I, observing him.

«Yes,» says he, looking a bit sheepish. «We thought we'd make sure that you really left.»

«Fair enough,» I answer. «And I hope it was a lot of trouble. I hope your cigar is a bad one. I hope it burns your nose. I hope you slip on the gang plank and fall in the water. I hope the Germans blow up your damned country. I—.» The second warning blows.

«Goodbye!» and inadvertently we shake hands.

Hawsers are slacked, cast off. The liner with its German spy steams off.

And that's the last I saw of war-time Newfoundland—and Newfoundland of me.

Now years have passed and Newfoundland at peace is as it must have been two hundred years ago. They speak the dialect of their forefathers, they believe in fairies and they shake their heads when they say «Good day.» «Good day, good day!» says everybody; and, at night, «Good night!» And if the wind howls down the street there's always a shelter where the warm sun shines deliciously; and there they are, the men of Newfoundland. «Good day! and how d'ye like the wind?» «I tell ye bye, it's not often ye'll see the like o' this.» «It's fine ye looked comin' into the harbor last evening! It's a grand little boat ye've got!» And when one said it was a number ten gale (though it wasn't) and another that the wind blew ninety miles an hour (it didn't), and one and another told us how there'd been a schooner in trouble and a rum runner in the offing and that no man for rescue or arrest would put to sea, the skipper looked properly proud, the mate looked nonchalant, and the cook noted it to serve up garnished to his readers.

"**H**OWEVER,**»** relates Robinson Crusoe (speaking of cooking) «he caused some Biscuit Cakes to be dipped in the Pot, and soften'd with the Liquor of the Meat, which they call Brews.»

In Newfoundland they soak hard-bread over night in water and then stew it with salt pork and salt cod. And that, terming it Brews, they hold to be their national dish. And, whether or not that dish has anything to do with the prevalence of Beri-beri among the poor in Newfoundland, it's good; and it became the international rough weather dish of the *Direction*.

But Newfoundland has more than medieval Brews. It has potatoes, turnips, cabbages and cod, and, as Mrs. Mary Tomas revealed to us, fat poultry.

* 34 *

Mrs. Mary Tomas's was not, we were later informed, the most select eating place of Channel. Traveling men (i.e. gentlemen) preferred the big house on the hill. Mrs. Tomas's was not a big house. It was a poor little weatherbeaten widow woman's home. We entered a low kitchen filled with the steam of stewing victuals and the friendliness of Mrs. Tomas. And there sat three big men dark against the daylight, come, like ourselves, for dinner. They were three skippers of three ships, wind-bound as we, and like us bound for Labrador; six men of liker purpose never met. And as common purpose, like common sorrow or joy, may be a common bond and leveler, so we discussed as one: first dinner; then the charts; and then, on board, the commonest, most vulgar, strong Jamaica Rum that the underworld of Channel could procure us or men drink—and live.

We were consulting charts. «*Don't*,» said one skipper, «don't start out in the strait unless you can make a harbor at night.» And the others nodded solemnly.

We were drinking rum. The skipper who had spoken warningly suddenly put his arm about Sam's shoulders. «Don't sail in the strait,» he said, «unless you can make a harbor at night.»

We were saying farewell. The few stars scarcely relieved the darkness of the night. Close to us lay the town, asleep. We shook hands and the dory pulled from our side. Then suddenly the rowing stopped and a voice spoke this: «Remember, byes, and make your port at night. Goodbye.»

For a long time we could hear the sound of the oars over the still harbor.

THE north wind left us; it had done its work. The air was sweet and crystal clear and from a cloudless sky the early morning sun shone peacefully on everything. It glistened on the sea and lured us there; it lighted up the land to look like summer; and over the snow banks in the hollows it cast concealing shadows. Trees could have only cloaked the country's loveliness or hidden the splendors of the sparkling town. So while the land called «Stay!» we sailed, waving farewell to the last fluttering handkerchief in the last dooryard of land's end.

Light variable breezes bore us westward and it was afternoon before we passed Cape Ray. But if calm had returned to more sheltered waters, here was a sea still agitated from the recent gale, heaving and restless as if the north wind's too swift violence had only awakened a desire that was torment. The wind came from astern and we rolled heavily. The land crept by as slowly as the sun.

Interminable hours somehow filled the day; and as the last tints of a golden sunset faded from the mountains we recalled a promise of the Channel skipper: «Fair weather on the western coast, no fog!»

THICK fog. Once in a while it lifts and shows a shore of mountain ranges. There's a forbidding glamour, a terribleness, about the scene. Whatever towns or farms there may be along this coast are hidden at the heads of bays; the solitude is unrelieved.

Into these mountains went, some years ago, a certain stranger, there in the wilderness to lose himself to men, to live and die. Of his continued existence there was no evidence except his rare appearances in town to buy provisions. He was known to be reserved but not unfriendly; and where he might have provoked the ridicule of the impertinent he at last won deference. Mad Hermit he was called; and it is probable that he was possessed by some subtle madness that might justify it. He was past middle age when

* 38 *

he first came to that region; and in the seven years until he was last seen he hardly changed. His beard and hair whitened and he acquired the ruddy tan of exposure; that was all. The fact of his death was established by some hunters who came, in the same hour, on his habitation and his remains.

His house or hut stood on a high promontory of the mountain side. It overlooked the sea. It was built of stones and turf and seemed of adequate construction to resist both the force of the wind and its penetrating winter cold. The interior was dark save for a small window seawards. In the recess of the window was built a table. There, over that, he lay, fallen forward on his outstretched arms.

There were few things in the hut, and nothing that could throw any light upon his identity. And not a book to serve as evidence perhaps, through what he read, of what he was.

It was inevitable that these mountains, in the aspect of peculiar grandeur and isolation that they this day wore, should recall to me that happening. I tell it here not only because I hold the memories and the reflections of a traveler to be essential to his narrative, but for the significance which, even before chance put me in possession of the story of the hermit's past, I, at once on hearing them, attached to those bare details of his existence and his death as I have told them.

And from what I now know I may add, with no improbability of truth, that by the fervent power of an imagination which had come to be his world, the hermit had conjured up in that last hour and moment that he lived so rich and exquisite an experience of happiness that, crying out, «Verweile doch! du bist so schön!»—with that will to immortality upon his lips!—he died, achieving it.

NO CHANGE: thick fog, fair wind; and a near mountain wall of shore—veiled as the presence of Jehovah. The compass was our eye by night and day.

We might have questioned the judgment that laid our course so near the shore. We didn't. The momentary glimpses of it thrilled us; we were there for that. But inasmuch as our being then just there so almost fatally concerned our now being here, we may, if we incline to reflection, read into it a lesson on the perpetual problem of being anywhere but as a means of moving on. «Live dangerously» might have been our motto. And in further token of it we set our spinnaker, in order, it might seem, that if we struck we'd strike all standing.

It was the end of my morning watch. We were in the vicinity

of Bonne Bay and logging five knots in a heavy sea. The skipper relieved me. The fog had lifted somewhat, revealing a far stretch of coast. Where this at its most distant point was silhouetted against the sky appeared a promontory that, unlike the nearer land masses, sloped seaward in a graceful, far-tending curve. It appeared lost in the murk of the horizon rather than ended there; so that either through the form's suggestion of continuance or by actual vision I concluded that land lay across our course; and with much conviction I called it to the attention of the skipper. He differed. The fog rolled in upon us and we held our course.

It was some hours later in the afternoon. I had come out of my forecastle to look at the fire and inspect the baking beans. «Good,» thought I as I licked the spoon, «but maybe a little more molasses.» So I added it. I looked at the clock. Only three-thirty! The beans would be done too soon. And just then the top of the companionway was pushed open.

«Cupid,» said the captain very quietly, «better come on deck and take in the spinnaker.»

I looked at the mate as he rolled heavily out of his berth and reached for his boots. There was a warning in the skipper's voice; I jumped for the deck. Thick fog, and wind; there, off the starboard bow a hundred yards away, the land!

The spinnaker crotch had been secured. Somehow we cast it off; we had to manoeuvre. It was a matter of few seconds; we had scant fifty to the land. We bore to port—a trifle.

«Rocks to port!» Steady. We'll pass between.

Then suddenly there loomed a line of reefs across that way; and everywhere except astern were rocks. A hunted animal cornered by dogs; we felt like it, we must have—though there was little thinking done of how we felt.

There were just two moves left; tiller hard down and chance to come in stays, or wear and risk the starboard reef by driving near it. Split seconds now. We wore. For an eternal instant we drove straight at the land. The reach of the mainsail fluttered. Then, caught aback, the mainsail filled, lifted the boom and hurled itself and everything to port. We trimmed sheet frantically, close. We gathered way. And the sea, lifting our wake, mingled it with the back wash of the surf.

Meanwhile the half lowered spinnaker was proclaiming confusion. We drew it, struggling, to the deck and bundled it; and all was trim. And as swiftly as the fog shut out the land we breathed again with the relief of danger passed.

«Listen! What's that?» It's nothing.

I am on the bowsprit. Listening. Peering into the obscurity of that fog with an intensity that is the sublimation of my fear. Listening to, to distinguish against the myriad noises of the silence, against the clamor of creakings and gurglings, of wind whisperings, of the beating of my heart, one fainter sound; peering to distinguish values in that grayness so fine that the mere blinking of my eyelashes is a rude disruption of the narrow scale.

Then suddenly, incredibly, a spot of lightness creeps into the plane of gray, a line of white—moving, and gone, and there again.

«Land on the starboard bow!»

We come about. The low reef drops astern. The fog encloses us. Anxiously we sail, in silence.

This time we hear it, booming; see it! «Land to port!—ahead!» Again about.

And always, standing there on the tip end of the bowsprit, seeing nothing of the management of the boat, having no bearing on anything, it is to me the wind that shifts and the land that comes toward me out of the fog, and retreats again. Lifted one moment high above the water, swiftly and gently lowered till my feet are touching it, soothingly swaying I seem rocked in space. A Heavenly movement! Like the dreams of ether it transcends the peril of the hour.

And that peril, the desperation of it since the first moment we encountered land, seemed by each futile tack to draw more closely and inevitably round us. Blindly we beat about beset by reefs and scarcely sea room for manoeuvring. We realized it. We were trapped.

And then it happened, when the intervals at which we met the land had become monotonous in their even recurrence, and sailing about at all seemed merely a senseless postponement of inevitable disaster, that as we peered and listened there came to us a sort of sensory annoyance as at the delaying of one beat in an established rhythm. The expected didn't happen. Slowly, not crediting our measurement of time, it dared to dawn on us that the whole thing was over. That we were clear of it. At sea!

Just so, not knowing how, great things like living on may come to pass. And we served grog to help us bear it.

«How about,» said the cook, sticking his head at this juncture out of the cabin, «a good, hot plate of beans?»

THE whale-back reefs had cured us of our interest in the land. Shunning that coast as if it had the power to pursue us, we laid a course that put us at the bright hour of sunrise so far at sea that not the highest peaks of any land disturbed the far, hard line of the gulf's horizon. Promptly then, upon the visual assurance that we were as if nowhere, the fog rolled in and the wind dropped out. And, with every reason to believe that we were now within the sphere of influence of the tidal current of the strait, the fairly definite position that dead reckoning had given us became hourly of less value. Enclosed, however, as we were, in fog, the warm blessing of the sun was not denied us; and we could lie upon a dripping deck and stare into a blue and cloudless upper sky.

And that's about all that we could do. For hours there was scarcely wind to give us steerage way; and when at last small ice bergs loomed out of the fog and passed us, that passing was so slow as to give no inkling of whether our progress absolute was east or west. «Cornbread,» reads the captain's log. «Wind over to W. by S. Ice. Cornbread. Thick weather.» Equal events in uneventfulness.

But even in the most dreary situation you keep your eyes on where you want to be. And so we kept *Direction's* nose at where we thought Belle Isle should lie.

"REMEMBER, byes, and make your port at night!» It was four o'clock in the afternoon. A change had come to wind and day. The fog that had lain so loosely upon the water was being pushed and rolled together, bundled, baled for transport. Ready! The wind came fresh from the northeast, put its shoulder under the cloud bales, lifted them. There, to starboard of us the long monotonous north shore of Newfoundland, to port the Labrador! With a precision compounded of our judgment and the grace of God we had entered the strait of Belleisle as fairly as though ice bergs had been channel buoys.

We spotted our position by the light house on Greenly Island; and, with four hours more of daylight, close trimmed our sails and made for Forteau Bay, the nearest windward port of Labrador. And as Newfoundland diminished astern the new land reared a long, low, sullen brow and frowned on us.

A brown land dark against the evening sky, treeless and immensely bleak; and the bared outcropping strata of the rock stood like a sea wall of coursed stone; of blocks so huge that, unconsciously conceiving of mankind by their scale, we found ourselves immeasurably small.

We entered the shadow of the land. It was cold. The sea and wind had risen. Night was not far off and Forteau Bay lay four miles to windward. Two miles to the westward was the harbor of Blanc Sablon, our logical port for the night. But the skipper had set his heart to windward, and that settled it. And for that the dawn searching about for us along the shores of Labrador did find us somewhere, we have those hands to thank that steered us out of what their young head got us into.

Two schooners passed us full before the wind for port. Their crews lined up along their rails and cheered us. Well they might!

ONLY four miles to go; course east, wind east northeast and blowing hard. And tide! We were to learn the force of that.

We had at first the happy thought of working along on short tacks under shelter of the land; *Direction*, never good to windward, made less leeway in calm water and a moderate breeze. We tried it. And during the hour and more that twilight lasted we came finally, through our repeated visits to the near vicinity of the shore, to be intimately familiar with about one hundred yards of its extent. We gazed at that cyclopean wall and marveled at it; and we saw in the stark hills above it the image of all desolation as some tortured mind might picture it. Not often is a view so barren as to invite no hope of anything beyond but more of that. Over those hills a line of tiny poles threaded its way to somewhere. We could even see the single wire up against the sky. So people live in Labrador! At the base of the sea wall, were piled and strewn great blocks of ice. There was one shaped to suggest a walrus. We came in the course of time to feel almost an affection for it. Sometimes as we'd return from our seaward tack we'd be a little ahead of it and sometimes a little behind. We were racing it—that stationary beast!

THE tide was against us. «Maybe,» we thought, «it's not so strong farther out.» The wind by now was blowing half a gale; and in the strait, broad open to the wide Atlantic, it had already raised a nasty sea, a short, mean chop that kept us drenched with spray. Now we were in for it.

A squall strikes and lays us on our beam ends. The sound of all the fury of it! of wind aloft; of seething water on a buried deck. The *look* of fury! of a ship laid over so that her shrouds to a man's height are carried under; of black seas bearing down; of lurid darkness, of churned white water hovering round; of being motionless in all of this. And then the vicious flapping of the reach as we luff up to ease her.

Too much! We reef—and that's no pastime. And the biting cold of the northeaster numbs our fingers.

Now Labrador is far away, but Forteau Bay marked by an unlit lighthouse on the eastern side is right abeam of us. We come about at last and run for it.

Time passes as before, tempestuously. The dark land looms over us; and at the water's edge the livid ice—great heaps of it, crowded up onto the rocks by the winter's jam and stranded there. And there, why sure enough! only a few yards off, our friend the walrus!

Now upon that we should, by every rule of common sense, have quickly turned our backs to the night's adventure and run up to Blanc Sablon to bed. But did we? No. Like dogged, valorous, undismayed, half-witted hearts of oak we put to sea again for Forteau Bay. And if I, for one, contrived to put on the manner of a sea lion, it was to mask the poor minnow's heart of me that, tired of fighting God, desired only in some sheltered cranny of the shore to sleep.

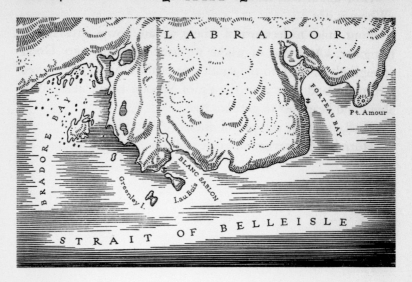

SAME night and scene. The same dark waters of the strait, but rougher; the same grim shore of Labrador, far off again, only revealed by that Point Armour light on Forteau Bay which now the lazy keeper has at last turned on; the same half gale grown older, stronger, surer of himself. Past midnight, and pitch darkness; not a star. The cook has gone below. Active confusion in the cabin: clothes, boots, books, crockery and the contents of the tool-chest all over the place. Cook at strange angle to floor is serving out hot lentil stew. (Rec. 2 cups lentils, ¼ cup rice, potatoes, carrots, onions. Boil slowly adding ingredients at proper intervals. Season; and then—happy thought!—just before serving, RUM. Magnificent.) Well—the cook is serving out the stew to the mate and skipper who in turn come down to eat it and get warm.

«How about that harbor to the westward?» says the captain. «Where is it?»

«Four miles to leeward of where we are now,» answers the navigator. «And two of where we were six hours ago. Good enough place. Keep to the south side of the channel till you see Greenly Island light over the tip of Woody Island; then come about and head east to get into it.»

«Well,» says the skipper, «I guess we'll go there.»

«Hurrah!» cry navigator, cook and foremast hand as one.

A S IF the furies rode our wake we now drove westward through that darkness. Soon we could see the contour of the land, blacker than night; the mainland long and low to starboard, and, off the port bow, the island looming large. Owing to sunken reefs and shoals the navigable channel between them was confined to a narrow passage close to the island's shore. Our speed as we entered the channel must have been seven knots; the illusions of the darkness doubled it. Suddenly from everywhere huge, livid, ghostly forms appeared around us; ice. We were powerless to check our speed or change the course; we bore straight at it.

The mate sprang to the bow. He screamed out, «For God's sake luff! Keep out of there! You can't—»

«Shut up,» said the skipper.

Close crowded as the bergs appeared, somewhere some passage opened just in time, and we drove through; and the white water of the ice surf churned around us. There were a hundred bergs, it seemed, pale green and livid in the darkness. I had my chart to watch; I ran below to hide my eyes a moment from the horror.

Then we passed through them so that again only the night confronted us, and the black lee shore. And all at once the light of Greenly Island broke from behind the island's hill. Now the fine moment of manœuvring was near! The land sloped gradually down—nearer and nearer to the water. It became a low spit almost indistinguishable against the black background of the sea. Where did it end! How could we get the bearing of the light! It was impossible. I waited until the land ahead loomed close. «Ready!» I called out, «Now!» We shot up into the wind. There was a wild fierce flapping of canvas, a whipping and slapping of foresail sheets along the deck, a furious clattering of blocks—a pandemonium of noise. She hovered there in stays. Then a big sea struck her starboard bow. She fell away again. We'd failed.

By the time we had gathered headway for a second try we were close to the lee shore of the mainland. Again we came up into the wind; again the furious clamor. And now, added to it, was the roar of the surf. The mate with his legs twisted around the port shrouds clung desperately to the struggling staysail sheet. A squall struck and hove us down to port; and the mate, still clinging to the staysail, was buried in the water to his neck. Again we'd failed.

We were now so close to the rocks that there was no room to wear. One hope was left: the anchor. Over and down it went, and ten fathoms of hawser followed it. It found bottom. We payed out two fathoms more. We held—and lay at anchor in a tide rip forty feet from a lee shore; a gale and a heavy sea. What next!

Now I possessed a certain pair of mittens on each of which was knit a heart. The skipper had worn those mittens that night; and I had somehow seen him in the flurry of the recent crisis pull one off and throw it on the deck. And the thought that it might wash overboard had tortured me. No sooner had we lowered sail than I contrived, carefully hiding my concern from the others, to look for it. I found it! And with that my soul was snug in port.

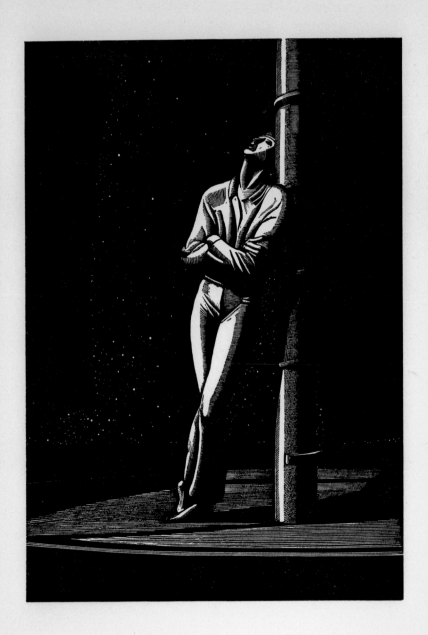

THE tide ran east and the gale blew west; the sound of torn and struggling water filled the night. Between the wind and current we swung broadside to them both and lay in miserable plight, spray drenched and wracked about. Here was no anchorage.

No sooner had we with numbed fingers furled the mainsail and cleared the deck of the loose ends of everything, than we weighed and in the still pitch darkness put to sea again; to sea with staysail set, westward before the wind with not a thought at first but to get out of what we'd gotten into.

Then almost suddenly the darkness grew less black, and day crept slowly up around us. We saw again that long, bleak, God-forsaken shore of Labrador; we saw ourselves, each other—

hollow-eyed, our boat and her white wake on the dark water. We saw the wind swept Gulf, green-gray and crested white, and ice bergs here and there, like flowers of an arctic wilderness. And now a hidden sunrise throws its shafts upon the belly of the clouds. Sunrise and storm; a leaden sky streaked with the pink of heated iron; and at a stroke the ice bergs burn a livid emerald and blue.

There is a village on a point of land, a loose cluster of houses and a spired church, forlorn and lifeless in that early dawn.

A sail! From the southwest a schooner under short canvas is working into Bradore Bay. We follow. Far in, near the head of the bay, close together like a sea fowl and its chick, we anchor side by side; and the long night is over.

ONE cold winter's day, years ago, in Maine, a boy came running to my house. «They want you,» he said, «to come up and blow out old Mrs. Smith's grave.»

Now I was a specialist, in those days, in making holes in the ground. I was a well digger. So I put on my mittens and cap, picked up my eight pound maul and a long drill, stuck a few sticks of dynamite and its accessories into my pocket and climbed the cemetery hill. There were my friends, the grave diggers, futilely picking at the frozen, gravelly soil.

«Let me show you!» said I. And while my partner, Hiram Cazalles, held the drill I drove it three feet into the ground.

I inserted the fuse in the cap, pinched the cap tight with my teeth, then tried to shove it into the dynamite. I couldn't. The dynamite was hard. But I made a hole in the dynamite with my pocket knife, put in the cap and fuse, cemented it with soap, lowered it into the hole and rammed it tight. I struck a match and lit the fuse. And we all retired a prudent way to watch the fireworks.

Seconds passed, a minute; two; then five. After an interminable period we all, with fear in our hearts, approached the grave again. «We'll try another,» said I.

Again it failed.

«Your dynamite,» said Ernest Wincapaw who had just come up, «is froze. Come down and we'll thaw it out.»

So we went to his trim little house and into the kitchen. There was his young wife frying doughnuts; and the children played about.

Ernest opened the oven door, put in the dynamite and shut the door again. Then we sat down and waited; and every move I made and word I spoke was studied for effect of calm.

That dynamite did explode—but not until we had safely planted it in Mrs. Smith's grave.

But to return to the kitchen; I had been educated in the romantic school; I believed that love and life and dynamite could not be trifled with; and I thought that putting dynamite into the oven meant only death. Did I then sit there, nonchalantly, awaiting an inevitable end? Nonsense, no! I knew from what I knew of the man, from what I knew he knew, that there was no danger. And such reliance—upon someone or something, upon God or luck or destiny or self—is behind most courage.

*   *   *

Now the events of the past forty hours had increased my respect for our skipper's seamanship and lowered my opinion of his judgment. Lowered it to the point that, valuing my life no more or less than most men, I ventured to address him somewhat as follows:

«Say, Sam! We've been almost wrecked twice in two days. That's too high a run of almosts. We want to get there—and get back.»

«I think so too,» said the skipper seriously.

At Bradore Bay is a post-office. «We'll be wrecked before we finish this trip,» I wrote—and tore the letter up.

ON BRADORE BAY is a little summer settlement of Labradormen. They live in houses, snug and warm. The kitchen and bedroom walls are gaily papered with newspaper supplements; the woodwork is painted with bright blue or red; the painted floors are spread with hooked rugs patterned with ships and dogs and birds. There is an anti-macassar on the rocking chair and a crocheted tidy on the table. The stove is bright, the pots and pans are shining. There is little in the houses; but what *is* there is theirs, home-made, for most, and savouring of home. They are poor people, mainly of French descent, of generations in this land. And they come from their inland frontier homes, men and women and children and dogs, late every spring to catch the seal and take up fishing for the summer.

Bradore Bay is a summer rendezvous for Newfoundland fishermen. Their schooners are anchored in a little basin in the midst of the Labradormen's settlement. They come from the great outside world; they have two pennies to the Labradormen's one; and they pronounce Blanc Sablon, Anse a Loup and Ile au Bois, Blank Salmon, Nancy Lou and Iley Bye. They hold themselves, therefore, to be superior to the Labradormen; and there's little friendliness between them. But for all that they're a good hearted, manly lot and no bit worse than their neighbors.

The settlement is on an island, a poor, treeless, unpretentious bit of land—and to us, released upon it from the confinement of the boat, all that dry land and native soil can be to man. Its little hills were mountains that we climbed to view the world; its narrow valleys gave shelter from the wind; its pools were lakes to bathe in—and how soft the moss under our bare feet!

Three nights we lay in the snug cove of the island. At first it rained and blew; and then the sun came out and it was calm. Two days we tried to sail. We'd get as far as a certain Bull Dog rock and there for hours slat about—so near to it at times that we were forced to use our oars to keep away from it. And with nightfall we'd drift home again and anchor in the basin. There we'd go visiting or be at home to callers.

And one night, memorable for conversation, there dined with us two captains, Andrews and Barbour of Trinity Bay. They told us, over our beans and rum, of the hard life of the seal fisheries of Newfoundland, of its dangers and disasters. And when they came to the tragic spring of 1914 I told my tale of what I knew of that as I remembered having written it. I have since found the story among my papers. It follows:

* 65 *

I HOLD a letter in my hand and read it.

Dearest: There's a blizzard raging here in New York and we are terrified to think of what you must be suffering in New-foundland. These few feet of snowfall and the zero cold that make so much misery here must mean mountains of snow for you and more intense cold than we know anything about. Be careful of yourself. Dress warmly.—Be sure to put on the bed socks and the woolen cap I made for you to wear at night.

Ha! I sit in the sunny, sheltered warmth of the doorstep of the old house I am rebuilding, and read these cautions—smilingly. The last of February—and in one day spring. The low sun shines almost from six to six. Daily it melts the snow and softens the brown earth. The brooks are full; they fill the air with their murmuring. Sea birds are singing. On my snug hillside facing south the spring has come!

Each day of March was like the first but maybe fairer. The sun dried the earth and brought out the green shoots of the grass in the wet lands. I left off my heavy hide boots and danced about light-shod. The house was nearly built and it was pretty to behold. I put a fence about it and a gateway arched over with the rib of a boat. And over the doorway I put a maiden carved in wood. She had been the figure head of an ancient vessel. Her hair was as black, her throat as white, and her cheeks as red as those of the fairest maiden of Newfoundland.

Men from up the harbor had come almost daily to visit me. Old men they mostly were, for the youth of the whole country were gone to the ice fields. They stood with me on the warm hillside and thought, perhaps, of their own youth, and told me what a place it was for courting in the springtime. «Wait 'til the byes come back from the ice; with them and the girls you'll have company enough.—This is the first place for dandelions—do you like them? Ah, 'tis a great sight they are, stretching everywhere right down to the water.» My house stood out of the town and looked somewhat back upon it over the harbor. I could see the schooners still quiet at their moorings where the bustle of prepa-ration for the Labrador would soon begin. Across the water I could see the counterpart of the hills on which I stood, but bleaker for they faced the north. Among the rocks of mine were bits of meadow land and on the pastures grew wild berries. There'd be crowds of youngsters to pick them when they ripened. My callers were kind and solicitous for my comfort. One brought me bread and cake and a rum-bottle full of cow's milk; another, two goat skins for mats on the floor; and a third, having heard that I slept on the bare boards while my bedding had not come, brought me, on his head, a feather bed and pillow, wrapped in a spare sail. I'm a wretched infidel, but Sunday nights I find myself comfortably at the church of the Methodists with Robert Percy, my carpenter and friend. After all, if one likes to go, why not? It is friendly there and the old hymns warm the heart.

Sunday night the twenty-ninth of March I went with Robert Percy to the Church of England, the church of my childhood, whose rector had officially called on me the day before and claimed me. This church was cozier than the great old tabernacle of the Methodists but it was awfully dull. It may be that the return of the young men from the ice fields will bring life to these services. We went out from the little church into the profound night. It was cold and the sky brilliantly starred. Over our left shoulders hung the new moon just setting. I thought it wonderfully beautiful. «That's a bad moon,» said Robert Percy. «We'll have weather, for you can hang a powder horn on it.» Sure enough the slender crescent lay almost fair on its back. I couldn't believe in the ill omen and questioned him. «I never knew it to fail,» he answered.

At his house we found the grandmother sitting alone in the kitchen. One child had gone to bed. The eldest was at church with her mother and the youngest, Grace, with dark hair and deep red cheeks, lay on the couch asleep. The grandmother made room for us before the stove. She is a singularly impressive woman. When she heard of the new moon that lay on his back she became serious. Robert Percy's wife soon returned and made us tea. I feast of an evening at her house; her bread is *so* good! and to my unfinished home a baker has yet to come.

Monday night as I went up the harbor I saw again, over the hill, the new moon. The air was even clearer than before but in spite of it there was an aura about the crescent. The whole body of the moon was visible, faintly illumined by the earth-light. I thought again of the omen of the hanging powder horn and it seemed incredible. We'll see, I said, and stepped into the long shadow of the hill. Wordsworth's «Strange fits of passion I have known» flashed to my mind.

I wake at six. I stick my nose and eyes out of my blankets and peer over the bulge of the feather bed to enquire the quality of the day. Through the upper sash of the little window, close beneath the eaves, I see the land across the harbor. If it be fair I know it before my eyes can focus on the far away illumined hills and houses for my room will be flooded with reflected sunlight. Tuesday morning, the last day of March, I looked, at six o'clock, through the three small panes of the upper sash into dull, blank grayness. I could only after a moment distinguish faintly the hills. Between, there fell a curtain of snow. I rose and lighted my fire and brought in coal, wood and water against the coming storm. The air was damp and icy; a strong wind had risen and was blowing the fine snow in gusts about the yard. My house is under the hill; no normal wind from North or East or West can touch it but in broken blasts. But, as the wind rose today and swept fiercely over the hills behind, it sought out every sheltered nook and, where it could not blow directly, penetrated by refraction. I could hear it from within doors about the chimney top; at first it made the fire roar, but finally entered the flue and blew the soft-coal smoke in clouds about the room. For an hour I stood it and then, taking from the mantel shelf my toothbrush, my razor, this tablet upon

* 69 *

which I'm now recording the event, and a volume called «*Old Faiths in New Light*» which the Methodist parson had advanced to me for my conversion, and stowing all the rest away from the reach of soot, I went up the harbor. Along the road I began to realize the gravity of the storm. The snow was already deep and drifting heavily. The wind at my back hurried me along recklessly, plunging me into drifts and becoming actually dangerous where the road hung on the cliff-side over the harbor fifty feet below. Near the town I saw a man coming toward me in the storm. He waited in a sheltered nook of the cliff. It was the shoemaker; he brought me my mended shoes done up in a red bandanna. I suspect the trip was undertaken as much with a view to a chat as for the delivery of the goods. So we talked for a quarter of an hour in the cleft of the rock. This man mended shoes, nets, barbered, did any sort of light work and got little for it. He showed me his pocket knife dented when he had fallen on a rock a year before, and sustained the hurt that had driven him to mending shoes. I spent the greater part of that day up the harbor. My dinner I had with Robert Percy and his family and repaid a bare spoonful of it by chopping up spruce boughs for the cow's bed. I returned to my house for a while in the afternoon though they begged me not to. Already the storm had risen to such height of fierceness that there was dread in everyone's demeanor and a desire to keep men indoors. It was a battle to reach the place; the wind took the breath from my nostrils and stung my face with driving snow. Look into it I could not, but glimpses I caught abroad, beyond the very track I strove to follow, were of whole banks of snow in mid-air carried by the gale. At the house I lit my stove but put it out again in haste for the kitchen had been blown full of smoke.

I abandoned the house and returned up the harbor before the wind. This was better. I looked as I went for the brooks that had murmured so pleasantly in the spring days just passed. They lay smothered under six feet of drifted snow.

I stamped and swept my feet in the Percy's hall. The people cried out with relief as I entered. To them all storms are ocean storms and they are terrible. I had never realized till that moment in the room that storm spells always death for some of the family of the followers of the sea.

In sealing, fortunes have been made. Towns have been built and have flourished with the dollars that the wooden fleets of old brought from the ice fields. They have decayed since steel and steam ruined their invested capital and built up the fleet of the merchants of St. John's. Men no longer take ship in their own harbors, but follow their captains to the metropolis to serve under them or where they may. Of the sailing fleet of St. John's were the steamers *Florizel* and *Stephano* of the *Red Cross Line*, the *Belleaventure* and the *Bonaventure*, the *Eric* that had been with Peary to the north, and the *Terra Nova* of the heroic Captain Scott, Shackelton's *Southern Cross*, the *Neptune*, *Viking*, *Newfoundland* and others. The ships are many but they can't hold all the army that journeys to St. John's. By rail, by boat, afoot, in hundreds they pour into the city. The streets are crowded with booted seamen. Berths are in demand. Tickets secured are marketable, and have been sold for five, for ten, for fifteen dollars. And I spoke with a man who, taken sick after securing his berth, had sold it for thirty-five dollars. This is half of all a man can make in his month of sealing. I had stood in the cable office at St. John's wiring to New York for my chest of tools. A seaman

was there. He handed his message to the operator to be counted,
—«Mrs. John Burns,» was read, «I have berth on *Southern Cross*,
sail tomorrow night.» «You're allowed one more word.» «Then
put 'Goodbye'» said the man.

I have not been to the ice but I believe that all men's work the
world over is alike in wearisomeness, for men are not braver nor
stronger here than there. For pay they receive a small part of the
value of their labor, for their risks nothing. So the dangers are
never counted. The fields of ice that float each spring through
the gulf of St. Lawrence and the Atlantic east of Newfoundland,
are the hunting grounds of seal killers. In early morning the crews
are set upon the ice. They wander the day long in quest of seals—
miles separate them from their ships. A man may break his leg in
the rough going, he may fall into the sea in crossing an open
space, the ice field splits and opens a gulf of water that bars return, or a snow storm rising shuts everything from view and
leaves the man alone and lost. The deaths in eighty years of
sealing have been many hundreds.

I stood in the kitchen and Robert Percy spoke,—«The *Southern
Cross* passed Channel Monday.» This struck the keynote of the
tension in the household; there was a murmur of sorrow. I
looked at each and felt at once the gravity of the tidings. «This
morning she passed St. Pierre and Michelon. It's a hard chance
she's got in this.» The gale was terrible; the frosted panes had
darkened the room and shut the storm from view, but the wind
howled dismally in the flue and the old house creaked in its timbers like an ancient ship. We all huddled about the stove, no
thought but of the storm and of the *Southern Cross*. The grandmother was remarkable. She had accepted the ship as lost from

the first tidings of her. The nobility of her mien had always impressed me. She was Grecian now in the austerity of her prophecy and grief. At tea time a man entered with news from the cable office. It was merely that no word had been heard of the missing ship. «It will pretty well clean out this place,» he said. The grandmother rose with a cry of pain and left the room.

That night I got up to go, but they would not hear of it. An old woman that I had never seen knew of my being there that afternoon. «Don't let that man go home,» she said. I am a new friend but if I had gone that night the women would not have slept. Nor would they let me lie on the couch in the kitchen. I went to bed with Robert Percy and saw and admired his old rose colored, home-knit drawers. A lamp burned all night on the hall floor and cast its light equally into all our bedrooms. In the hall the old clock struck the hours and half hours as the ship's bell sounds them.

Wednesday morning the wind blew unabated, but from the Westward. The aspect of the day was the same as yesterday; we could only guess that above the gray and drifting clouds of snow there was a fair sky. I went to find my house. It was there, of course, but hardly to be seen from far. The drifts upon the way were beyond belief, and at the house so coated were the windows as to make it dark within, almost to the need of lamplight. And my brook! Even the sloping valley sides were gone, filled level with the land above. One day had plunged us into deepest winter. Without water I could not comfortably live, so again I returned to the harbor. As I came up the road toward Percy's house I saw a knot of men about the door. The horror of the news they told, my God! I shall never forget. Last night the entire crew of the

* 73 *

steamer *Newfoundland,* one hundred and sixty men, had frozen to death on the ice.

We can know little of such a death. At the store later that morning a man told this story. In 1898 he had gone to the ice. They entered the harbor of St. John's exulting in the sure hope of first arrival. But there before them at the wharf stood the tall masts of a sealer; they were beaten. They came to anchor and sent ashore the bos'n and a small crew. The speaker was among them. As they neared the wharf he saw it to be crowded with men and that some carried their arms or legs in bandages. From the ship there were being borne frozen corpses. The bodies were mostly naked, stripped at death to save their comrades. They were in all attitudes, crouching, doubled up and straight, wide-eyed as if living, and grimacing. They were being chopped from a pile of ice aft on the vessel's deck. Forty-eight had perished from this ship—the *Greenland.*

Wednesday night I slept again with Robert Percy. It blew a gale and the night was thick with snow. I would have returned to my house for I had tried the road. But people were unnerved by now. Thursday and Friday and Saturday passed. The weather was still severe. I dug into the drift and found water. I was out of coal and dragged a sackful laboriously over the snow from the town. All day of every day the cable office up the harbor was crowded with people. The reports were posted as they came; children acting as messengers copied them and carried them back. Survivors there proved to be of the *Newfoundland* and the list of perished fell to half the original report. It was still appalling beyond belief. But still of the *Southern Cross* no news was heard. The St. John's papers published a list of her officers and crew;

they numbered upwards of one hundred and seventy. One pointed out to me the homes of some of these. The dread of the loss of this steamer had passed almost to certainty and the mention of the house, the wife, the children, the hopes and ambitions of any of those on her became a tragedy. The drama written in the loss of a hundred men is a world story. It includes all; mother-love, the tale of courtship, of youth, of marriage—it touches the whole gamut of emotion in ten thousand lives. The pastor visited the wife and daughter of the master of the *Southern Cross*. The wife had cried to exhaustion and the girl lay in half delirium calling for her father. This household was demoralized and little food had one tasted the week. On Tuesday the house had been swept and made ready for the father's return. That was the day that others knew that it would never be. There was another house where little food had been tasted those many days for poverty. A mother lay sick in bed of the birth of a seven months' child, that she had borne unattended. She had many small children and no grown person with her. The loss of the *Southern Cross* would drive her insane for her mind was weak and wandered at child birth.

The news that came on Saturday night was of a three masted ship seen in Placentia Bay and thought to be the *Southern Cross*. The message came privately to the druggist who was told to hold it until confirmation. So it flew like wildfire through the town and to the stricken homes. Before an hour it was contradicted, for the sighted ship was not the *Southern Cross*. This news was brought to us at the Percy home. On the *Southern Cross* they had no near relation, but grief among these people is not alone for those they are connected with. The mother had gone at the first news to the Master's wife and child. She returned crestfallen.

There had been many at the house and though the callers soon learned of the denial of the rumor they had left the poor wife clinging to her hope. As the evening wore on and no word came she began to fear again and wept, begging to be told the truth. How terrible false hopes can be! Another woman, we were told, clung in her extremity to her belief in the unseen spirit of the dead. She cried, «I can't believe it for I have seen no token!» Can there be truth in tokens? In 1872 the *Village Bell* was at the ice. One night the wife of a man aboard her awoke. She heard the tramp of men on the street from the shore. They bore on their shoulders her husband's chest. At her gate they put it down heavily. She sprang from bed, went to the door and opened it. The night was empty of men and of sound and no chest was there. That night her husband and seventeen others perished on the ice. Another woman whose man was lost returning from the Labrador longed for a token. She rose each night and taking his clothes from the chest went about the house calling to him. «Would you speak to your husband if he came that way in the night?» asked someone among us. «I'd be afeared to!» said Robert's young wife, tensely. They spoke again of the unhappy wife and daughter and asked the grandmother, who was of distant kin, if she would visit them on the morrow. «No,» she answered. «I called today. I told the girl she had lost as fine a father as there ever lived, but 'twas the will of God.»

It is Monday the sixth of April, and the sun shines at last with the balm of returning spring. I stood naked out of doors at sunrise and felt its warmth, while my ears were filled with the sound of dripping snow. In a few days the last traces of this second winter will have disappeared from the land; the grass will resume

* 76 *

its growing, the ancient lilac bush its budding, and one may look forward to the promised dandelions of June. The town across the harbor will appear again as serene and beautiful as on the spring morning of a week ago. Through the seasons forever it will turn its weatherbeaten face stolidly seaward and show, save in the gradual decay of its might, nothing of the calamities that have struck its heart.

APROPOS of the maiden that adorned the doorway of my house in Newfoundland I have this, bitterly, to add: I found her in 1914, weatherbeaten and neglected in the rubbish heap of a ship store. I took her, washed her, scraped and sandpapered her. I painted her skin white, with roses in her cheeks; I dyed her hair a lustrous black. I gave her a necklace and earrings of gold. And I set her up where every man might look at her.

Then, when at last I left her country, I wanted to take her with me. I offered what I could for her. But I was poor and it was little. So I left her there.

Then ten years passed. And one day having entered on some business a smart antique shop in New York, there, hardly changed,

I found her. Out from among rare cabinets and chairs and clocks and porcelains, the frayed and mellowed chattels of decayed gentility, she stared—that sailor's sweetheart—vacantly, as if the room, the city and the world were part of the wide sea and firmament that she was born to. And as I turned and ran to her, and sweet memories and almost love crowded and clamored in my brain and breast, as I reached out to touch her as I used to— suddenly I dared not. And I knew what changes time and affluence had wrought. And I reproached myself.

«Where did you find her?» I asked the salesman in a whisper.

«In Boston,» he whispered back.

So then—not even asking what her city price might be—I tiptoed out.

BUT there was another occurrence, that night of story telling over beans and rum, which was of such sinister suggestiveness, and which might have led to such tragic consequences in the later course of our voyage, that, unsolved as it remained, I may only, as in the first chapters of a mystery story, state the facts and review in brief the particular circumstances attending them.

My preparation to be navigator for the voyage had been, of necessity, of the most hurried order. In the little spare time at my disposal before sailing I had tried to master a few of those simpler problems which, in my judgment, would suffice for the emergency; and for the understanding of these I did review and come to fairly understand the elements of spherical geometry upon which their formulæ are built. Not daring to trust entirely to my memory, nor caring to stoop to cribbing from the text-book, I had condensed and arranged the formulæ to my own liking, and written them into a note-book. Then, to give this note-book the dignity of a manual, I had covered it, in true seaman's fashion, with oil-cloth.

The first trial of my new learned art had resulted, as I have recorded, in an error of which I was sufficiently ashamed; and I had subsequently, on every fair occasion that offered, practiced and tested myself until at last, in the idle hours of drifting about on Bradore Bay, I could with absolute precision observe the sun and the sea and prove, however one might doubt it, that we were in fact on Bradore Bay. And, using my oil-cloth-covered note-book for all my calculations, having even devised the method of working on tracing paper over the formulæ written there, it must have appeared that my practice of navigation *depended* on that magic book.

It may seem that the appointment as navigator of one so inexperienced was rash—especially in view of the eminent qualifications, to accept his own estimate, of the mate. «I have read,» said the mate pompously, «every book on navigation that there is.»

«You don't *read* books on navigation,» I cried indignantly, «any more than you *read* arithmetics. You *study* them.»

It so happened that my first triumph of accuracy came on the day of the recorded captains' dinner. It was a perfect day, cloudless and calm and clear, and our progress happily was such that our position at noon was identical with our position at four o'clock. I took my time. I shot the sun at calculated noon; at four or thereabouts I caught it in my mirror and brought it slowly down until it kissed the sea—and caught that instant like a movie censor. I made my calculations—faultlessly.

I wrote on a slip of paper: «June 28th. Position at 4 P.M. Lat. 51° 28′ 35″ N. Long. 57° 13′ 41″ W.,» and slapped it onto the chart table. «Try that!» I said; and I carried my precious note book back to its exact place fourth from the left in the row of ten books on my forecastle shelf.

«We are,» said the captain after a few moments plotting on the chart, «just about to run on to the Bull Dog. Get out the oars.»

There was a lot of drinking that night. For reasons of my own I left the party when the two skippers retired—and went to bed. I slept as only a pure heart and rum can let one.

I came out in the morning to a scene of carnage. Broken glass was everywhere, and even the chimney of the high swinging lamp had crashed before some gesture.

That day we sailed. It was a fair day so I took a sight. I went to the shelf for my note book. It was gone. And though I searched those narrow quarters hours on end for days it was never seen again.

Who took it?

AT 2:30 in the afternoon we left our anchorage. We didn't
sail out, we were towed. Tired of waiting for a wind,
ashamed of inaction, embarrassed by abortive leave
takings, we wanted only to get out of it and off to sea.
Near the mouth of the bay there's a pleasant little isle named
Paraquet. There, protected by the might and majesty of the
Dominion of Canada, the quaintest of small sea birds love and
make their home. It is the puffin's paradise. Abreast of that we
drank the stirrup cup with Captain Barbour. «Good luck!
Goodbye!» A light breeze lifted us, we gathered way; and once
again our world of human kind was we.

Then that light breeze became a wind; and as the afternoon
wore on dark clouds obscured the blue and threatened heavy

weather. Two sperm whales breached to leeward. On a rising Northeaster we ran into St. Clair Bay and came to anchor off the settlement. We'd learned caution.

God what a place! A round bay, open to the south and every wind and sea the south might send; unbroken shores; a bowl, rock sided, steep but where a dreary valley led to the vaster dreariness of the continent. On the rock-terraced hillside facing north straggled the houses, weather-beaten wood, stark, flimsy; stick fences; tottering wharves and fish houses strewn at the water's edge like driftwood crates left stranded by the storm;—a dire epitome by man of nature's ugliness; the whole an ugliness so unrelieved by any little, lovely, kindly thing that it became through all its elements in sum as the refinement of desolation absolute. And louder than the clamor of the wind rose from the shore the howling of a hundred dogs.

Then came the men in boats to see us, crowded on board and came below to visit. They filled the cabin, standing or sitting awkwardly on awkward seats, caps in their hands, hands resting on their knees. And these men, sons of sons of generations here, born here to live and die in St. Clair Bay, to never see a tree or train or city or cultivated field, or anything through all their lives but this, were—just like other men, only a little shy. But how endure it!

And the next day, Sunday, we went visiting about on shore. How poor the people were! how clean and neat and snug, how comfortable with home-made things their houses. Suddenly, as I walked along the path I saw a girl's face at a window—just for a moment. I was ashamed to stare. And oh, I thought, how beautiful it would be to live here, and never go away—forever!

That evening a young man came on board. His eyes were weak from snow blindness; they troubled him. We gave him boric acid as a wash. He was a fine, good-looking fellow.

«Are you married?» I asked.

«No,» he said, «there aren't many girls about here.»

I said to him: «There's a girl living in that square house just above the turn of the path. If I were a young fellow I wouldn't rest night or day until I got her.»

«Ah, well,» he said, «there's plenty of time.»

The Northeaster raged all day and night till Monday afternoon; then it dropped out. It cleared a little and a light breeze came out of the northwest. We sailed. And I thought how never again I should see the girl in the square house at the turn of the path.

HARDLY had we cleared the mouth of St. Clair Bay than the fog enclosed us; and, by the obscurity of that, with variable winds and calm, with strong currents that we couldn't calculate, we entered upon eighteen interminable hours of blind-man's-buff, with ice and rocks as hazards and only luck to keep us clear of them. Some hours after the fog had shut down, the lazy keeper of Cape Armour station stretched himself and set his wheels to turn; and the far off dreary bellow of the diaphone accompanied throughout my watch the drearier murmuring of rain. Slowly we drifted round and round with only now and then a puff of wind to straighten us upon our course. And then toward midnight a prolonged near roar as if of breakers burst upon us frighteningly. We could at last attribute it to a tide-rip on the western side of Forteau Bay, and know by that that we had reached the point where we had hoped to be one night a week before!

So (to find a lesson in that last week's night's experience)—if one's maintenance *in statu quo* may be expressed by the equation $a+b+G=X$ (in which a and b are one's inherent endurance and power, G is God, and X is the sum of all the forces of the Devil) we have only to find a moment of which the equation discounts G or multiplies the X—or, better, both—to have the formula for getting on. Thus life becomes quite simple—if we'll but grow intimate with God and Devil.

But fog upsets all reckonings, and we emerged into the morning without a notion—east or west or, within limits, north or south—of where we were.

«We've drifted to the south-westward,» said the mate, «and are back in the Gulf of St. Lawrence.»

But while none of us was inclined to claim much progress, that was an outlook far too gloomy for our hopeful hearts to entertain; and, with the wind become both fair and steady, and the warm sun shining on us and our vapor shrouded sea, we sailed east cheerily, ready for any revelation of good fortune but that astounding one which God, as if by Gabriel, announced to us. For suddenly there came to our ears, simultaneously from east and west, the far off trumpetings—we'll call them that—of fog signals. Fast, as we listened breathlessly to comprehend so weird a happening, they neared us, always by chance so mingled as to baffle our efforts to identify them. Then came the sound of rushing water, near to us, invisible; and with one nearest, deafening blast a steamer loomed upon us from the fog astern—immense and terrible to us so little in our little craft. Parting the seas to stream behind her in a turgid wake, she passed. The fog closed in, her blasts grew fainter and were lost. We were alone again, rocking a little to the steamer's swell. And from abeam to starboard came, steady and clear, the deep-toned nasal roar of a diaphone. Cape Norman! We had passed the Strait.

The fog lifted. We saw the white tower of the light, the red roofed signal house, Belle Isle, the open sea.

Fair wind—and forty miles to Battle Harbour!

NEAR the southeastern corner of Labrador, a little north of that indefinite point where the Strait of Belle Isle becomes the Atlantic Ocean, lies Caribou Island. Off the northwest corner of that, so close to it that only a bare hundred yards of water at the widest, and a few feet at the narrowest, separate it from the mainland of Caribou, is Battle Island. The narrow gut is Battle Harbour; and the settlement is built along its Battle Island shore.

The day held beautiful and clear; the fair wind carried us by afternoon close to the Labrador. For hours there unrolled for our delight the long, wild panorama of that coast, transformed by the low sunlight into a wonderland of beauty. And at last, just as the long shadows of the mountains claimed us, and the cold of approaching twilight settled on us, just as a port, hot supper and a quiet night were what we wanted most, there, under our nose, appeared the slim back door to Battle Harbour. And yet so narrow was that passage that we could never have attempted it but for the friendliness of a fisherman who at that moment happened along.

«Come aboard!» we cried.

And ten minutes later, towed by his motor boat, we steamed into the road of Battle Harbour, dropped our anchor and sat down to hot, Alaskan sour-dough pancakes and coffee.

"THE Samoan Islands, the natives and their habits, have been so often described that I omit that part, and proceed with my voyage." That, written by the venturesome Captain Voss in the book of his voyages, shall serve to spare the reader all that might be said of Battle Harbour, its natives, industries, wharfs, fish flakes, stores and store rooms and the Grenfell Mission. So much, one might add, has been written of hospitality, of the comforts of civilization, of friends, of the delight in all of that by cuffed and battered wanderers, as to permit no telling of it even in subjective narrative. So very much, in fact, has been written about everything that—if we but face the full significance of wise old Captain Voss's words—all honest writers may well lay down their pens and, assuming that everything possible has been done toward the promotion of that universal human understanding which is the premise of social happiness, settle down like common mortals to the cultivation and enjoyment of its fruits. It is, however, upon the assumption of their *un*common mortality that writers proceed; and it is thus that the whole clap-trap of art becomes a broadcast of assumed peculiarity or self expression. Let me, in the rôle of writer, put on this mantle of my own contriving, and, content enough with my own average share of common greatness, display, rather for sympathy than praise, the meaner me.

I didn't like the mate. I didn't like his looks, his size, his shape. I didn't like the way he moved, the way he spoke. God! that self-sufficient unarticulated drawl! that music of a dull, stale, undigested-fact-encumbered mind! Navigator! «Journalist,» by his passport, «student»! Student of what? Iguanodon of the Riviera bestirring itself to park its cumbrous bulk on anything. Incongruous cuckoo of our nest, a vast voluptuary pampered, housed and fed at others' cost.

«I'm fed up with it,» said I to the skipper. «For two weeks I have cooked every meal but three and washed all the dishes. I've done every bit of work on the boat but the deck work, and I've done my share of that. And I've stood my full watches.»

«That's true,» said the captain a bit guiltily. And he reflected a moment.

«Suppose we shorten your watches.»

«No,» I said, «I want my full watches.»

So it was arranged like this: I was to be cook; the other two should share the scullion's job. And thereafter, whatever my spiritual pleasurings might have been, martyrdom was not one of them. And if, consequently, there was often a pail of dirty dishes kicking about twenty-three and one-half hours out of twenty-four, it was no concern of mine, nor, since the skipper eventually washed them, any concern whatever of the mate's. Only once did the cook have the grim pleasure of summoning all hands to dinner, seeing them well seated with napkins, as it were, tucked under their chins, and lips all moistened toward the savory feast, to cry, «Well, pass your plates»—when every plate and saucer, knife and fork and spoon lay dirty in a pail on deck.

It is July the fourth. For two days we've been idle—with a strong head wind to justify us. We hope to make a start this night. All is on board, of odds and ends of reprovisioning, but coal and water. The fetching of that having been assigned to the mate, the skipper and I do it.

On the wharf there stands a tall, spare, white bearded man wearing a blue officer's cap—Captain Moses Bartlett of Brigus, Newfoundland! I run and shake my old friend by the hand.

«You've changed terribly,» he says, «grown old.»

I look hard at him, and for pity can only answer, «You're looking young and well as ever!»

«Your boat,» he says, «is too heavy rigged. She must roll something awful.» He's right.

He continued. «The thing to look out for, now, is the ice. When you leave here go up the coast as far as Round Hill Island; then steer your great circle course for Greenland.»

IN THE half light of the early morning of July the fifth all hands bestirred themselves, got up; we came on deck. It was cold. The silent town lay dark against the eastern sky; the land was black, and stranded bergs glowed pale against it. Clear heavens strewn with stars, and a fair wind S. by W.!

Noiselessly, as if stealing away, we hoisted sail, weighed anchor and bore out. And so, without tumult and the clamor of leave takings, quietly as the coming dawn, we entered the solitude of the ocean.

And if we were not annihilated by the contemplation of such vast adventure it was by grace of that wise providence of man's nature which, to preserve his reason, lets him be thoughtless before immensity.

* 96 *

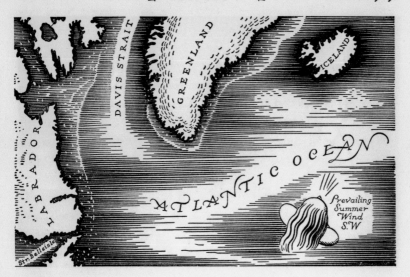

THAT *reason*, meanwhile, occupied itself with the immediate problems of the voyage and fed upon the facts of
land and sea and wind as they not only displayed themselves each hour but as their nature, history and habits
were recorded in the pilot guide and chart.

Generally speaking, the hazards of that crossing were actually
neither more nor less to us, with our equipment, than they had
been to Leif Ericsson almost a thousand years before. Our boat
was possibly more seaworthy; Leif's was larger. We had only
sails; Leif's ship had sails and power; and whether the auxiliary
be of motor or of men they must rate alike as factors in safe
navigation. We had the compass; Leif the polar star and sun—
and all the wisdom of experience and tradition to read them by.

* 97 *

They served him well enough. And if against two untried sailors and a sea-cook we weigh the thirty-five sea-hardened Norsemen of Leif's ship, we may well choose, if we must cross Davis Strait, to sail with Leif.

Every spring releases from the Arctic waters west of Greenland a vast quantity of floe, pack-ice and bergs to be swept southward along the shores of Labrador and Newfoundland. Through June and into July it haunts that coast, crowding the land or carried seaward as the wind blows west or east. It forms throughout its season an impenetrable barrier between Labrador and the open sea.

Down the east coast of Greenland flows a polar current. Rounding Cape Farewell it flows west and north almost to Godthaab, hugging the shore, jamming that shore with ice from the last of March through August, not only closing the southern ports to navigation but presenting a danger as real as if the reefs and headlands of that coast were floating at the whim of wind and current.

It was our problem to avoid both the Labrador ice and the «storis»—as the Greenland ice is named. And to that end, taking advantage of the free water along the Labrador coast which the recent South-west winds had given us, our course lay north for eighty miles to Round Hill Island; thence north by east for Godthaab. And, if the sun would shine by day, and stars and moon through the short hour of the night, if the wind held fair, if ice would only browse in its appointed pastures, then quicker— in view of eternity—than we could say Robinson Crusoe would we be in Godthaab. And so we were. But how!

For we knew, thanks to our charts, exactly—to the minutest contour of the shore and sounding of the waters—where we were going, and exactly—in degrees, minutes and seconds of latitude and longitude—on which of the 16,600,160,000 intersections of the screen of our earth-consciousness lay the very iron ring-bolt to which we should by God's sweet mercy and the Dane's indulgence tie.

And because in knowing *that* we knew what Leif knew not we were to him as gods to men.

SOON, as we sailed northward that fair morning of the fifth, the near land which the risen sun made golden brown receded to become a range of blue and distant peaks. Then these became as islands and at last—farewell America!—were lost.

A freshening wind, full sail with spinnaker, we logged six knots for hours; then came fog.

Nightfall and eight o'clock; I took the helm. Figuring that we had put Round Hill Island abeam we laid the course for Godthaab, N. by E.

Then the wind dropped, and in an hour it was calm; and not a living sound, no little gurglings and murmurings of moving water, nor whispering in the shrouds, entered the stillness—only the listless, lifeless creakings of an inert ship. And neither light nor darkness was around me; only a murk, sullen and ominous. Then in the north a huge brown cloudbank formed itself, and grew until it overspread and filled the sky. A wind puff struck us, jibing the boom. Now it has come! I thought.

How calm it was again, how hideous with threat! Stealthily, as if manoeuvring for one, sure, terrible, annihilating stroke that red-brown darkness gathered and enveloped me, crowded upon me smothering my sight. God it was dark—and still! I could have screamed for horror of it, shrieked into the silence to tear it and precipitate whatever cataclysm it so long held back.

It breathed again and the main boom crashed back to starboard. Then suddenly a miracle of gentleness occurred: as if in pity of my utter littleness and fear, so helpless on so wide an ocean, the horror wept, and the tear-drops fell as rain over the water and on me. So, as if the darkness and I wept together, passed the hours until midnight; then—my watch over—sleep.

THE second day! Cloudless; and from the west a light breeze until noon; then it died out. Sunshine and calm; and one could never have believed in cold or storm, it was so quiet—and so dull. The afternoon passed into evening and the evening into the deepening twilight of the night, my watch. Scarcely a breath of wind, and all sails set in supplication for it.

Conditions so far had been favorable to solar observations, although never throughout the voyage could I, during the hours of my night watch, see the Polar star. Invariably, as the darkness came, the sky was overcast with fog or cloud; and instead of exulting in the splendor of starlit heavens I shivered through interminable hours in the contemplation of nothing at all, yet ever straining my mind toward the annihilation of time and the achievement of some helpful disbelief in the reality of my bodily misery. It was cold—oh, bitterly! Dress as we would—and we soon learned the art of wearing all we owned, layer upon layer of clothes put on in order of their size; appear at last, each man to take his watch, bolstered and comfortered and slicker coated, happy and warm; sit down in the narrow cockpit, light the pipe, incline the mind to ease and profitable thought—and in one hour the damp chill air had penetrated to the marrow of the bone; and the moment, and the hour, and life became a torment to endure. Daytime was different; there was always something to divert the mind. Even the bow wave and the wake showed a recurrent rhythm and a patterning of foam that pleased the eyes and lent each moment entity in a visible kaleidoscope of time.

Of talk there was little; of conversation none. And I no more ruthlessly dismiss from consideration my shipmates' tiresome gossip about yachts and yachting than I would all possible discussion by me of the length and quality of hog's bristles in a painter's brush. If anyone on board had wit or wisdom he concealed it; and as to those personal confessions that might have proved such hazards to enforced companionship there were, beyond the mate's beach-combings from the Riviera, fortunately none.

There was one argument.

«When I say North,» said the mate, «I mean where the compass points.»

«When I say North,» I answered, «I mean North.»

At the end of three quarters of an hour it was terrific.

«How like a miserable, lazy sensualist that is—to confuse a

local loadstone with the polar north, to revolve your earth around some little variable spot of attraction! Only the wind is labeled by magnetic points. Wind-bag! Balloon!»

All this I was about to say when the skipper, sensing murder, interposed and settled it with: «Both are right! now keep her N. E. by ½ E.» I did. And we held merrily on our course, close hauled, for Godthaab, N. by E.

TIME was eliminating one worry from our thoughts, the Labrador ice. And when, during the morning of July 7th we passed through scattered bergs and into ice free seas again we felt assured of having left that risk behind.

The breeze was now N. W. and moderate; we made good progress. My observations for position showed us to be drifting to the eastward farther than the skipper's dead reckoning calculations allowed. And if the chart showed two diverging courses penciled on it, that merely expressed a wise precaution against such error as faulty chronometers might have tricked a navigator into. However, with the wind steadily inclining northward we sailed as close hauled as allowed of progress.

At 5:40 P.M. of the seventh I made my last observation for longitude. It put us 53° 33′ 15″ W.

On the following day there was a good horizon for the sun at noon. It gave 57° 15′ 17″ N.

From there on we sailed blindfold.

THE eighth was cold and dirty. Toward night it breezed up strong from W. by N.; a short, high, nasty sea was stirring and there was every indication of bad weather. Sensing it, I asked for a reefed mainsail as I went on watch. We didn't reef.

Under full sail we carried on, rail under; tossed by disordered seas, dipping our prow to lift it streaming to the clouds while shattered water beat like shrapnel on the drum tight sails. Spray-drenched—and dry; no weight of water ever touched the deck. There was no danger, ever.

Only the too easily imagined horror that one of us, alone on deck at night, the cabin shut, the men asleep below, might somehow, moving to secure a flying rope end or to trim a sail, slip or be caught off balance. And never in the pandemonium of wind and sea would his small cry be heard.

It had been proposed that the helmsman secure a rope about himself. One day we tried it—and then gave it up. The risk was easier.

We did rig stationary life lines fore and aft; and these remained throughout the voyage. And often it came over me, in contrast to the almost carelessness of my own movements along the narrow deck, how balanced, poised, we lived between an upper and a nether infinite, the rail a tight-rope over the abyss.

It is 2 A.M. of that night; the skipper's watch. Wind E. S. E. Mainsail is double reefed. An hour later and we're hove to under staysail; a bad sea and a moderate gale.

Daylight; still blowing hard although the worst is past. Reefed mainsail on again at 5:30. Leeway, and little progress. In the afternoon we set the jib. The wind died down, became a light and favorable breeze. But the sea remained confused and agitated. It kept its running start for what was coming. So between threat and promise ended July the ninth, fifth day at sea.

NOW the wind came from the south, a gentle wind. We set the spinnaker. But the sea had raised itself against us and resolved its dissonances into a consistent swell that rolled upon us from the north by east. Then it came on to blow.

The great spinnaker, bellying like an old maid's petticoat in a gale, lifted and fought, straining at its slender sheet and lashings. Its boom jaw cracked. No matter; it still held.

By ten in the morning we had stowed it.

By noon the wind had risen to half a gale; still we held on; full sail.

The skipper's watch; wind forty miles or more; full sail; we're logging five, six knots.

＊ III ＊

The sea becomes a fury and the wind a gale. She plunges, deep; and lifts—so prettily!—and broken seas go streaming over her.

Six, seven knots. Still carry on! Too long.

Suddenly there's but one thing to do; and quick. We heave her to. Braced in the chains, dipped in green water to his waist, lifted all streaming out of it—to plunge again, the mate secures the jib. The mainsail fights us like a living thing gone mad; four thousand pounds of fury against thirty fingers. Inch by inch we win, and lash it tight.

*   *   *

The cabin of a small boat at sea, hove to in a gale of wind. All hands below. Mess and confusion, wet and cold, and semi-darkness from the closed companionway. Skipper and mate wedged in their tilted berths; the cook, braced 'thwartship on the floor, reads «*Ann Veronica*» aloud.

A COAL stove in a gale at sea! May God have mercy on the man who thought of it. Light it—and puff! Smoke belches from the open drafts; from every seam flames jet as from a blow torch. Then it is out; and you stand at the dripping companionway gasping for air.

Again: you remove the coal and the charred kindling with your hands; put in more newspaper; whittle a piece of soft pine into shavings; add them; select and stack on top the choicest, driest, lightest kindling; omitting coal this time, pour over all a quarter cup of kerosene, and light again. Whew how it roars! Then suddenly the whole accumulation of that flaming moment, flame and smoke, and soot, explodes into the room like dragon's breath, a smoke screen, tear gas, flammenwerfer rolled in one, one last breath-stifling touch to misery.

Events *too* bad are good. And one may some day learn, in honoring those factors that have made us men, to put the last straw first. The coal stove would *not* burn. Almost, if oil stoves had not yet been made, they had been thought of there and then. We fortunately had one.

And soon, with the Primus nailed to the floor, with the stew gurgling pleasantly over its flame, with the cook holding the pot steady with one hand and his book with the other, Ann Veronica went sweetly on her way annoying us.

OVE to throughout the early morning watch. Thick weather; heavy sea; the wind is moderating. The skipper, cleaning the cabin, drying the saturated clothes by a hot fire in the stove that by some mystery of nature draws, pokes his head now and again into the air and sniffs the day. Decidedly; the gale is past.

By sunrise we are under way again with main and staysail. Fire below, fair wind and daylight. We're wallowing in a heavy sea somewhere in Davis Strait, fog bound but on our course; and moving. All is well.

It is the middle of my morning watch. We roll and yaw; the gaff is thrashing viciously. Then—crack! The heavy jaw is splintered.

We heave to and lower the mainsail without mishap. And for four hours I work to make a new and *better* jaw out of the spare tiller that we carried.

And it was of great personal satisfaction to the ship's carpenter that—having once observed the mate, work-minded for a moment, put back the tools on noticing that no one had sharpened them for him—he could now say, as he roughed out the new jaw with the axe, «Mate, sharpen the chisels!» And the mate did.

So, just because the boat rocked a little, the acting cook that noon hurled a dozen eggs, in the form of two oath-seasoned Riviera omelettes, into the coal scuttle before producing a third for us to eat.

Five in the afternoon; a strong beam wind, thick fog, an oily swell. Suddenly, incredibly, near to us to weather a gray steam trawler looms—and is lost again.

Land? And how far?

THE wind which in the night had headed us backed in the early morning into N.N.W., then swung to North. The fog was thick. Just after noon small ice appeared, and the water assumed the color of milky jade as when glacial streams are poured into the sea.

Then came two little birds and flew about us; and, as though dropped by them, rock weed like olive branches floated by. Then land!—so suddenly! looming so swiftly on us to leeward and ahead. Reefs and dark island masses, spectral in the fog—whose curtain seemed that moment more to hide a certainty of shipwreck than a promised land.

Nearer. Like an enraged animal it showed its teeth; and the white foam of madness was around them. Then, even before the echoes of our first «Land Ho!» had died, we came about, and fled.

THESE were cold hours, cold days and nights that we beat up that coast. The sea was icy and a thick, wet fog hung round us always. Sometimes the sun would shine down brightly on our dripping deck, cold light rays from a cloudless sky; the fog that lay upon the water became dazzling bright—and more impenetrable to the eyes than ever.

We had now been five days without observation for position and were relying on dead-reckoning. That, with head winds and the recent gale as factors, could offer no more than the probability that we were somewhere south of Godthaab. But where, exactly, and whether or not before the fog should lift we'd have sailed north too far, we had no way of knowing.

To navigators approaching Greenland for the first time the

outlying reefs and islands of the southwestern coast, and the mountain contours, are so uniformly continuous as to present a serious problem in identification. And so generously, as with a pepper shaker, has the hand of the Almighty bestowed his hazards that you may properly hesitate at attempting to make port in thick weather. Nor was the aspect of the land as we had seen it such as to invite mariners to partake of its shelter and comforts: low reefs and towering islands of rock whose steep sides offered little hope of landing and whose treeless summits robbed that hope of reason.

The thirteenth gave us a two-reef breeze, more than we cared for with our port likely as not abeam of us. But we jogged in and out keeping sharp look-out on our landward tack. And often, before the land revealed itself, we had passed behind innumerable islands which, as we came about, lay straight across our seaward course.

Fortunately we had continuous daylight. And when during the hours of my watch that night we lay utterly becalmed, I secured the boom amidships, lashed the tiller, and sat—bundled with blankets and my legs down the warm companionway—reading until midnight.

IT BREEZED up early in the morning from the south, and we stood in again toward the land. The fog, denser than ever, had cast a pall of twilight over the water and narrowed the visibility to scant two hundred yards. Suddenly a mass of rock loomed close aboard; then more, to port and starboard, everywhere. We ran the gauntlet of them working back to sea.

But the thing was getting on our nerves. No sooner had we fled from the too stark reality of the land but we must put back again to try somehow to end the irksomeness of getting nowhere. Prudence is a virtue that soon stales.

It was an hour past noon and had begun to blow. We lowered jib and main-sail and proceeded down wind under staysail toward the land, fired with the first real determination—kindled, I think, by shame—to bring the situation to an issue. And fate was with us.

We seemed, as we advanced, to be emerging from the fog into an area of clearer atmosphere. Our senses somehow caught the subtle change before the realization of it dawned; and into that grimness which had been our mood crept presently an almost exultant expectancy as though we should for certainty at last and now behold the glamorous country that we'd climbed the latitudes to reach.

And then it came—not suddenly, nor close, nor frighteningly, but gradually from a long way off, low islands and a long low coast, gray in a silver mist. And as we stared, it all at once grew bright, and shafts of sunlight streamed down through the mist illuminating patches of the land and the white surf along its shore. And the mist drew back and hung as a great wall of steel gray cloud behind the mountainous land. «And this is Greenland,» we thought, «so wild and beautiful!»

And yet the clouds were even then resolving into forms so lofty as to dwarf the land and draw our eyes to watch their evolution from dense fog to masses every moment more compact and mountainlike. Then, after an instant when the illusion of high ranges was complete but for the too fantastic altitude of the cloud pinnacles, our doubt of the incredible gave way and we sat staring speechlessly at a blue barrier of granite mountains rising to cloud-wreathed, snow-topped peaks four thousand feet and more above the sea.

Between the summits, here and there, appeared the far, white snowfield of the inland ice. Glaciers curved stream-like down steep valleys or hung suspended on the mountain sides. Granite and ice; and over the stony hills of the broad foreland sparse vegetation turning green with summer.

And with the knowledge of being at last at the threshold of Greenland came, momentously, the question *where!*

CHARTS have the same relation to the geography of the mariner's visual experience as four-dimensional geometry has to the problems of everyday life: they picture in two dimensions what to the eye at sea appears in one. Those most fantastic indentations and projections of the shore on which the navigator would depend to get his bearings show as the straight unbroken line of where the sea's plain cuts the land. No wonder then that with the panorama of that coast before our eyes and every promise on the chart of here and there a settlement and everywhere, almost, a bay or anchorage, we were as lost as if no charts had ever been.

But, just as upon our determination to make the land there had followed that spectacular unveiling of it, so now in our most need to know our whereabouts the sun came out; and in that moment the heavy fog that lay over the sea lifted and revealed for the first time in days a clear horizon.

I jump for the sextant. Braced in the halyards—for the boat is rolling heavily—I catch the sun and draw it downward toward the western ocean rim.

The mate stands by the chronometer.

«Ready!» I call.

The seconds pass. The crimson sun declines toward an emerald sea; nearer and nearer. «Now!» I cry.

And the mate writes on a slip of paper: 3 h. 47 m. 23.9 s.

And even as I leave the deck the day grows dark again.

It's latitude we need; the sight and calculations are for longitude. I figure carefully. With longitude 51° 35′ 11″ West as the result, I go to the chart. Assuming us to be three miles from the shore I draw the line of our course. The intersection of that with the line of longitude gives our position. We're less than fifty miles from Godthaab!

I T SEEMED, perhaps, too good to be quite true. Certainly
the prompt abandon with which all responsibility for our
course was forthwith thrust upon me smacked somewhat
of a taunt to do or die; while the name Godthaab Kent with
which I was threatened was somehow to be the symbol of that
everlasting disgrace which must attend my life if now in stating
our position I was wrong.

Our narrative approaches so near to its catastrophe that every
happening and almost every thought assumes distinction as con-
tributing somehow to our being finally where drama needed us.
Bearing in mind accordingly that interest in detail which the High
Court in Admiralty for Southern Greenland might in its later
investigation have shown—and, graciously, did not—we enter

upon such solemn detailing of little events as only those impressed by knowledge of their aftermath may value.

We had been at least two hours on our course for Godthaab when we sighted the first evidence that we were approaching the region of a settlement: there on the summit of a little island stood a cross-shaped beacon.

Two courses, by the chart, now lay before us: the open sea to Godthaab, and an inside passage between successive islands and the mainland. The outside course was longer, and dirty weather was in prospect. That way, however, was my choice; and being then at the tiller I headed seawards.

The skipper and mate were at the charts.

«If we're approaching Godthaab, as you say,» spoke the skipper, «can't we take this inside passage?»

«We can—but—»

«Then that's what we'll do,» he said.

We headed in.

Putting a cluster of islands with beacons on them to port we entered sheltered waters. Here was less wind; and the surface of the bay, save for the little ripples of the breeze, was as smooth as a fresh-water pond. How sweet it was to sail so evenly, so quietly, and hear again those liquid gurglings on our sides! And see the land again so near! To feel the friendliness of that majestic wilderness, its peacefulness—immense, secure! But a few hours more and we'd go sailing into Godthaab, and drop anchor! And the people would crowd the shores to greet us! How wonderful you are, they'd say! They'd come aboard to see the ship and marvel at it. How small, how strong, how clean and neat and beautiful! How brave you are! And the men—even the hardy

Danes—would admire and envy us; and the girls—sweet, gentle, blue-eyed Danish girls—they'd *love* us!

«Clean up!» think I.

«More speed!» says the skipper. And he gets out the spinnaker.

«For God's sake, don't put that on,» I protest.

Great headlands frown upon us. Inlets with canyon walls point like the outspread fingers of a hand toward that arctic rookery of storm, the inland ice. Alaska, Cape Horn; brothers to here: I've felt the violence of their sudden squalls, those dreaded «wullys»; how with malignant fury they strike down from mountain heights, lashing the sea to foam; so swift, and terrible!

We set the spinnaker. The wind, as if to shame my fear dropped to a gentle breeze.

«Keep on this course,» say I, «until you have that hive shaped island fair abeam; then bear off sharp to port.» And I go below to cook supper and put everything in order.

It was a splendid supper I prepared that night: corn bread and corned-beef hash and pancakes. And it was with some thought of the scrutiny of Danish housewives that I meanwhile set about that scouring and scrubbing which our long days and nights at sea had put us in such need of. So time passed.

Meanwhile the wind had headed us a bit. This had entailed a change of course and a departure from those simple and, as I now know, correct sailing directions which had been my last word. I was called on deck—only to look upon strange land forms and to share in the general confusion as to where, exactly, we had got to.

But if our course appeared now far from clear it was of no immediate concern; the breeze was failing us. It was nighttime and the sky was so heavily overcast that twilight darkness was around us. A most gentle rain began to fall.

The skipper headed for a small fiord that lay before us. On a faint breeze that scarcely gave us headway, in silence so profound that it became the murmur of the rain, we turned the headland flanking its approach and entered. And all at once, as one—there between mountain walls, sheltered and peaceful, awed by the scale and stillness of that solitude—we knew that rarest and most simple wish: here, for a time so long that it has only a beginning, merely to live!

Just where we anchored I shall never know; we were a long time about it. The sandy bottom of the fiord shoaled rapidly toward the head; and once we gently ran aground. But we poled off to some sufficient depth near to the southern shore. Down in the cabin I took the anchor's splash as signal to serve supper.

How warm and neat and clean they found the cabin! Dressed for port. Port! And tonight we sleep!

«And as late as we want to in the morning,» added the skipper.

But, for an hour after the others had gone to bed, I sat in my trim little fo'castle writing those pages of my diary which should have been these; writing through that grateful, midnight calm and stillness while the rain fell gently on the deck.

And of much that being there at last, in port in Greenland, meant to me, the last line that I wrote may speak: «Tomorrow,» it read, «I paint!»

THE motion woke me. Where was I? I remembered. Daylight came but faintly through the fo'castle ports, shadowed as they were by the dinghy. My clock showed ten-thirty. How I had slept!

We were rolling violently; a sudden roll, a lurch to starboard. I heard steps on deck, voices, the sound of hawser paying out. Oh, well, we're at anchor; and no one has called. I braced my knees against the side board of the bunk; I had need to.

Suddenly we were careened so far that I was almost catapulted onto the floor. I got out, dressed hastily and opened the door into the cabin. It was broad daylight there. The skipper was in bed.

«She's drifting with both anchors,» called the mate from deck.

«Give 'em more rope,» answered the skipper.

I reached the ladder. At that moment something rolled us over, far, far down, and held us there; and the green sea came pouring in as if to fill the ship.

«Damn it!» I cried, «and I'd made everything so neat!»

On deck a hurricane; I'd never felt such wind before. The sea was beaten flat, with every wave crest shorn and whipped to smoke; cold spray and stinging rain drove over us.

I helped the mate. «We'll need the third anchor,» I said, and started aft.

The skipper appeared. «Good, get it out,» he said as I passed him. I went below for the last time.

The spare anchor was knocked down and stowed under the coal sacks and provisions in the after hold; it was not easy to come at. Removing the companion ladder I set to work. Hard work it was, cramped in that narrow space on hands and knees. As I dragged the hundred pound sacks out onto the cabin floor—always, strangely, careful not to damage anything—I'd look up and see the gray sky through the opening above my head. Then one time glancing up I saw the brow of the mountain; and always after that more mountain showed and less sky. And at last the mountain side itself seemed to have moved against the ship and to be towering over it.

I had laid a lighted cigarette carefully upon the chart table; this, as I worked, was always in my mind—that it should not be left to burn the wood. And so, from time to time, I'd move it just a bit. We were so careful of our boat, to mar it in no way!

But all the while I had been shifting goods and moving sacks of coal; so that at last I came to the anchor. It was a large anchor and very heavy. I dragged it out into the cabin.

«Come,» I called to the mate, «and help me get this thing on deck.» And as I looked up I saw the mate in his yellow oilskins, bright against the near dark mountain side.

«Not much use now,» said the mate; but he came down.

It was hard work to lift that anchor up, and we seemed not to be very strong. «I lose my strength from excitement,» said the mate. I thought that I did too—but I didn't say so.

We lifted the cumbersome affair head high and tumbled it out into the cockpit. As I started to follow, a great sea lifted us and rolled us over; I hung on, half out of the cabin. And I stared straight at an oncoming wall of rock so near astern it seemed about to crush us. The sea rose high against it, and broke and became churned water that seethed around us. It cradled us and lowered us gently; and the dark land drew quietly away.

Then came another sea that hurled us and the land together. «Now for the crash!» I thought—and I gripped hard and braced myself against it, and watched the moment—thrilled by its impending horror.

There was no crash—that time. Ever so gently, just as we seemed to draw away again, our stern post touched the ledge; so lightly touched it that it made no sound, only a little tremor. And the tremor ran through the iron keel and the oak, and through the ribs and planking, and through every bolt and nail, through every fibre of the boat and us. Maybe we had not known that the end had come; now, as if God whispered it, we knew.

So for a third time we were floated back.

Then, as if the furies of the sea and wind were freed at last to end their coquetry, they lifted us—high, high above the ledge—and dropped us there. And the impact of that shock was only less than those that followed for that half an hour until *Direction* sank.

THAT half an hour! We lay, caught in the angle of a giant step of rock, keel on the tread and starboard side against the riser; held there by wind and sea; held there to lift and pound; to lift so buoyantly on every wave; to drop— crashing our thirteen iron-shod tons on granite. Lift and pound! There the perfection of our ship revealed itself; only, that having struck just once, she ever lived, a ship, to lift and strike again.

A giant sledge hammer striking a granite mountain; a hollow hammer; and within it a man. Picture yourself the man. I stayed below, and was.

See me as Adam; set full blown into that pandemonium of force, his world—of wind, storm, snow, rain, hail, lightning and thunder, earthquake and flood, hunger and cold, and the huge

* 132 *

terrifying presence of the unknown—using his little wit toward self containedness against the too-much of immensity; and quietly —for Adam lived—doing the little first-at-hands one on another in their natural course, thinking but little and reflecting less. Adam and Man; and me in that compacted miniature of man's universe, the cabin of the yacht *Direction* on the rocks of Greenland.

We live less by imagination than despite it.

MATCHES: They're in the fo'castle cupboard. I get out a lot. Next: Keep 'em dry. A big tin on the shelf. Lentils! I pour them out on the floor;—no, not all; we don't need all that room for matches. Pack in matches, put on the cover. Good. Now something to put the tin into. Sam's little bag lying there; the very thing! Good neckties and white collars! Out with them!

Put in the tin of matches; add odds and ends of food; close it; that's done.

Kerosene: Five-gallon tin too big to get ashore. The one-gallon. Buried under stores.

Over the coal sacks into the after storage space. God what a mess! Dig in the stores; dig—and find it. Good!

Alcohol for priming: Find it—a small bottle.

And the Primus stove? Crushed on the floor.

There's another in my pack-sack with pup tent, nest of pots, etc. Under the starboard fo'castle bunk. Smothered under spare sails, spare rope, spare clothes, painting supplies. Out with everything. Ha! the sack!

Flour, rice, butter, beans, dried soups, coffee, bacon, chocolate, cigarettes: fill up the sack with them. Done.

Chronometers, the beauties! I take them from their boxes and wrap them carefully in layer on layer of clothes. I partly fill a duffle bag with blankets; put in watches; add the sextant, my silver flute, my movie camera, more blankets.

And this and all the rest, plus now and then a garment or a blanket, I pass on deck to the mate.

«Enough!» I think, with pride.

«Come out of there,» calls the mate for the fourth time, peering down into the havoc of that hold.

Havoc! It's no-man's land; a mass of wreckage: doors, drawers, shelves, sheathing, stove lids, pots and pans and crockery, springs, mattresses, tools, beans and butter and books,—torn, splintered, crashed and mashed, lifted and churned and hurled again with every shivering impact of the ship.

Over my writing table in the fo'castle, nailed to a timber, was my sweetheart's picture. I had not forgotten it. I will take that picture, I had thought, tuck it for safety next my skin; and carry it, last thing, ashore with me. Then on my return I'll say, «Look, darling, what I have brought home!» And I'll take the picture from over my heart and show it to her. And with not so much modesty as to hide my valor I'll tell how in that hour of confusion and terror I had thought of her. And what a fine fellow I shall be!

So I now clambered, somehow, back to the fo'castle; found her image looking out serenely over the carnage; took her down and tucked her next to me; put an envelope containing my money, my passport and my permit to land in Greenland next to me too; and—wading, climbing, dodging, holding on for dear life—made my way out and to the deck.

THE mate, working like ten stevedores, was getting things to shore. It was not far: a jump from deck to rocks, jump on a rising sea and scramble out of it and up before that step of rock was flooded. Hurling a sack, he'd follow it; clutch it and drag it to the safety of a higher ledge.

The sack containing the chronometers rolled back into the water. It was retrieved intact. Some things, washed from the rocks, were lost. The tide was littered with our gear and goods.

The thrashing of the main boom added confusion to the deck. Only the too stout standing rigging saved the mast.

The skipper was on shore desperately struggling to secure a mast-head line to a great boulder. Finished on board I leaped to help him. The yawing mast-head tore the line away from us each time we'd nearly made it fast. But once as the mast leant far down toward us we got two turns of line around the rock; we braced ourselves and held. The three-inch cable snapped like grocer's twine!

Direction's end was near. Quickly undoing the sack I got out the movie camera. Listen! Even above the noise of sea and wind and rain I hear for a short minute its small whirring like the beating of a heart. And by that sound, what happened there, in Karajak Fiord in Greenland, at eleven in the morning of July 15th, 1929, achieved soundless immortality.

END OF PART I

II

WEST GREENLAND, mountainous and wild. A raging storm; cold rain in torrents from low hanging clouds. Streams pouring down the mountain side are turned to vapor by the gale; and the whole face of nature, land and sea, smokes as from internal fires.

Across the rough, grass matted foreland between sea and mountain move three figures, men; the only living things in all that wilderness. Leaning against the wind they labor on.

They climb a rise of land; and from its ridge look down into a sheltered basin. There lies a lake round as the moon. Its pebbly shore shows smooth and clean and bright against the deep green water. They descend to it and, standing there, look over at the mountain wall that bounds it. The dark cliff rises sheer from lake to sky. From its high edge pours a torrent. And the gale, lifting that torrent in mid-air, disperses it in smoke.

The three men stand there looking at it all: at the mountains, at the smoking waterfall, at the dark green lake with wind puffs silvering its plain, at the flowers that fringe the pebbly shore and star the banks. And at last one of them speaks.

«It's right,» he says, «that we should pay for beautiful things. And being here in this spot, now, is worth traveling a thousand miles for, and all that that has cost us. Maybe we have lived only to be here now.»

AFTER some preliminary exploration of the immediate wilderness in which we found ourselves, we returned to the vicinity of the wreck and chose a spot for the erection of a temporary shelter. An overhanging cliff that faced to leeward offered itself as one side of such a tent as we could complete with the spinnaker. After contriving to secure the canvas to the land above, despite much hindrance by the wind, we drew it down and weighted it with rocks. And although the floor was too uneven and encumbered with boulders to permit of much comfort we found fair shelter from the wind and rain, and ample space for the assembling of our small store of worldly goods. These precious goods we proceeded to carry over; and it was our good fortune that the wind, which still raged unabated, now helped our tired backs to bear their saturated loads.

Soon, however, I set about preparing dinner, for we had been so far that day without a meal. And as, presently, we sprawled about in the orange twilight of our rock and canvas home, and sipped hot soup from scalding metal cups, and nibbled chocolate and wet hard-bread, it may have been that childhood memories stirred in us without our knowing it, memories of some house contrived with shawls over a table top, the glamorous light of that, the far away contentment of some special day when, being children, poor and free, we played that we were robbers or ship-wrecked men: here, at any rate, we were, shipwrecked and poor; and the warm golden light of the wet canvas was on us and on our goods that lay spread out like robbers' booty all around us; and if ever in this so-called vale of tears men can be happy we there, that hour, were.

IT WAS once, not very long ago, my earnest intention to submit to the authorities of the great Guggenheim Foundation a plan for the sending of me at random round about the world to search among the rich and poor, the wise and foolish, good and bad, among the whites and reds and browns and blacks and yellows everywhere, for what made people happy. Only, I think, when I read of the financing of a scholar to study what was called the Graveyard Poetry of England, did I realize that all men must make their quest of happiness alone.

Now it was only a little while after that sweet hour in Greenland of which I have told that we bestirred ourselves from our contentment and visited the wreck again. Some hours had passed, the tide had fallen; and although the gale still raged and the sea ran high, it was clear to us that the boat would remain on the ledge and even be, at low tide, partly out of water.

She appeared to have been completely gutted, not only of those articles of her contents as would float but of all such woodwork as formed no integral part of her frame. The forecastle hatch now stood uncovered and every sea came spouting through it like a geyser, bearing each time some quaint contribution to the picturesque assortment that littered the rocks and water. Books, paper, painting canvas, shoes, socks, eggs, potatoes: we fished up what we could.

«I've got a book!» cried the mate, wielding a long pole like a fishing rod and throwing his catch high on the rocks. He recovered it.

«*The Triumph of Death*!» he read aloud.

Of the long diary of our trip that I had written, only one page was found, the last: «And tomorrow I paint!» I read again. And knowing that all the wherewithal for that most probably was lost I thought how little—pictures and diaries and books and all that kind of thing—amounted to.

But it was clear to us that we must eventually recover no small part of what remained on board. And whether it was the thought that these promised riches made us that moment relatively poor, or that this lavish increment to our supplies robbed what I'd done in saving things of its heroic flavor, something destructive of my own late perfect happiness had entered. And so, instead of dreaming of life there for weeks or for a season, I came to have no thought but how to leave that place.

I T WAS approaching midnight. Among the boulders that lay heaped at the foot of the cliff that sheltered our camp burned a great fire. Its light falling luridly upon the nearer objects deepened the gloom of the surrounding wilderness and hid the storm. Blankets and clothes were hung about the blaze to dry; they made a wall against the night, and stopped the puffs of wind that found their way around the cliff; and while one side of the blankets steamed in the heat, the outer side became quite saturated by the drifting rain spray. But it was warm there at the fireside; and although the others still were busy at the wreck, there I sat huddled against a rock, privileged to dry myself and rest.

The few reflections that I did allow myself during that part of an hour of self-engendered coma were of so pleasant a nature as to make their concealment from my companions imperative. A shipwreck is after all one of those occasions which, like death, impose upon us, as gentlemen and heroes, the observance of a mien of suffering fortitude, of tragedy redeemed and ennobled by courage. We may not weep; yet must our smile, if we incline to smile, be so gracefully tempered with the mark of effort as to leave no question of an underlying misery of soul. It was my secret shame that I rejoiced.

I had rejoiced, a little, even as we lay there pounding on the rocks; there, like an evil voice, my own, «You're glad!» was whispered to me. And though for decency I fought it down, it was the truth—that thought—sinful and true; and doubly powered it lived on and worked within me, grew. And as I sat there by the fireside it flowered; and I dared to look at it and call it me.

So when in a little while the others came back from the wreck bringing with them more pathetic, salvaged things I said: «How wonderful!»—and only thought how tasteless fate had been to rob us thus of our disaster's fine completeness.

But now, with one o'clock, the hour of my liberation from such disheartening dedramatization of tragedy has come. Already, despite the storm, gray daylight creeps over the mountains, and reveals again that dreary wilderness and the far-extending broken line of shore along which I look forward, hopefully, to plod my way.

My pack-sack is ready. It contains: food for a week; a tent; spare socks; a sweater; a Primus stove; a cooking pot and a cup; two blankets; a large and cumbersome boat compass. The outfit is heavy, fifty pounds at least, for its contents are wet. I raise it onto my shoulders and put the tump-line over my forehead. Ready.

Prayer is a useful thing—as ritual. We need such ritual. Prayer is self measurement—for God's delight. My ritual centered upon my chronometers. They were very beautiful chronometers—loaned to me by their famous makers. They had been on other voyages and served great navigators. The chronometer is an instrument for measuring God in terms of time—for man's small need and pleasure. «Remember,» I said to the mate, «to wind the chronometers at noon.»

And to those who value prayer I may proclaim that not until I reached Denmark two months later were those watches left to stop.

STARTING off at a merry pace, lightly leaping the tussocks of that boggy land, dancing along and singing, I came in no time to where the land dipped down. Here at the edge I turned for a last look behind me. How far I'd come! There was the fire, a tiny star in the half light of that hour; and standing on the rocks two little figures waving goodbye. «Goodbye!» And I plunge down the ravine to the river's edge.

The little river is swift and deep. I dare not cross it there. I follow it up stream.

I come presently to the round lake that we had seen before; the river is its overflow. It is wider and shallower here. I start to ford it and the water rises to my boot tops. Those rubber boots are my only footgear and I will not fill them at the commencement of my journey. I return to the shore and undress. It is raining; and here where it is sheltered are mosquitoes—thick. Rather than risk everything at one time in the swift current of the stream I first carry the pack-sack over. The water rises to my waist—no higher, fortunately. But it is icy cold. When I have returned and fetched my clothes I pull my wet clothes onto my wet body, shoulder my pack again and march. But I am no longer singing.

The coast must be my guide so I return to it. But now the land is steeper; it is hilly, rough and boggy. Traveling is difficult. And the land forms are so huge and simple as to deceive the eye: what seems a little way proves long. I feel myself suddenly to be a very small creature creeping ever so slowly over a vast terrain.

Yet it is profoundly moving in its grandeur! I look down upon the dark, storm-swept fiord, and at the farther mountains looming immense through the gray veil of rain; and I look upward at near mountains towering over me with here and there such glimpses of snow and ice as to suggest that in that region it is still winter. But underfoot is long green grass matted by wind and rain; and every-where are bright flowers. And the thought comes to me to pick the flowers as I go, and gather them into a bouquet for my sweetheart; it would be so curious a thing to do! So I begin to pick them.

And from that moment the gathering of those wild flowers be-comes to me a fixed idea, a purpose to my being there more real and tangible and, strangely, more important than my journey's goal. So, as through those long heart-breaking hours I plod on, I'll often leave my path to pick some new bright specimen, and add it to my growing handful. Oh there are lots of people who go through life like that—clutching bunches of wild flowers in their hands.

I STROVE to follow the shore, and yet its steepness drove me always farther inland. At last I stood on the bare rock ledge of an important rise that I'd laboriously climbed, and looked far down on sea-invaded flats. Here was a new detour! And that indented, broken, hilly, mountainous coast beyond held little promise of good going. Discouraged for a moment and tired, I crouched in the shelter of a boulder—to rest, to eat some chocolate, and to read my chart.

And yet there was little in that chart that I could not have memorized. Assuming that we had been wrecked in Karajak Fiord we were now less than thirty miles by sea from Godthaab, yet out of reach of Godthaab overland. On the point of that peninsula on which we found ourselves the chart indicated a settlement. But of the nature of that settlement, winter or all-year-round, it told us nothing. And we had read too much of the ancient migratory habits of the Greenland natives and too little of their stable modern ways to feel assured of finding people at the spot named Narsak on the chart.

But whether or not there was really a Narsak could, I had figured, be soon known, for by the chart it lay but eight miles from our camp. Therefore—to settle that, to learn beyond a doubt our whereabouts, to find some way of getting out of a predicament that had at last somehow to be gotten out of—I'm standing on a Greenland hill-top in the pouring rain, with my house and a week's provisions on my back. And if I am a bit refreshed by the few minutes' rest and the bite to eat that I have had, my mind is far from cheered by that most dreary landscape now confronting me.

DREARY! To tell about it as I came to know it, feel it, step by step over the winding, weary miles I made of it; down hillsides steep and slippery or strewn with shale and boulders, or intercepted by ravines and sheer descents; down, down to those sea-flooded flats to wade and wallow through them laden and heavy shod; to search the shores of deep rain-swollen torrents for some place to cross, to wade them or to hazard leaping with my load from slimy rock to rock; to climb more hillsides to avoid some bog or pond; plod miles to gain a hundred rods; all this what use to tell about but to convey some sense of the interminable hours and miles I walked, and of the utter weariness that came to me.

Now I have wandered inland; the way is mountainous and I am

off my course. Down to the sea again to try a plain that lures me. Good! it is firm and smooth. With strength renewed I stride along.

Then suddenly it ends with a sheer drop to a deep inlet of the sea. Following that inlet to its head I come to where between steep canyon walls a cataract pours in; I follow that up stream. At last I come to a place where it seems possible to cross. I shed my pack and carefully investigate each foothold, plan each step and place to jump. It *can* be done. And if I slip and fall it is all over —forever! I think about it. And then, wearily and with some shame, I lift my pack again and shoulder it, and heavily continue on my inland way.

And yet if I had known where that at last would lead me I might have dared the leap.

IT IS hours later; evening, I judge. I am on a high plateau in the midst of minor mountain peaks. It is cold up here and desolate. Snow lies on the northern slopes; there's little vegetation anywhere, just rock. It rains unceasingly; and the whole face of nature streams with water. How have I come here? Why?

I followed the tortuous windings of that cataract till it became a river, deep and wide. Still following along low marshy banks I came at last to a broad lake that spread behind me back along the way I'd come. I followed it. Then, where it seemed to end, a small gorge interposed through which from higher land another lake poured in. At last I circumnavigated all and reached the shore of the first lake again. It was firm going there. «Soon I'll be round it!» I rejoiced.

But at one spot a mountain spur reached out and rested in the lake. Straight from deep water it stood up, a wall of rock. «Oh I can never go back all those miles!» I thought. And so instead of starting on a long, safe, gradual ascent I climbed it there.

Maybe nothing that I shall have to do in all my life will approach in toil my climbing of that little mountain side; I was so tired! It was the pack that made it difficult. I couldn't bear it on my back; its weight would overbalance me. I dragged it. I'd get a foothold and then pull it up; and hang it for a moment on some little point of rock while I again found foothold. Or sometimes I'd deposit it upon a ledge above me and climb up to it. And once I tossed it up beyond my reach—to find I couldn't climb there! So I went round about and came toward it from above, where, reaching down, I just could capture it. «What,» I sometimes thought, «if it should escape me and roll down again! I never could go back for it.»

And the foolish idea came to me that I with my burden was Christian. And that all this journey with its labors, roundabouts and hazards was contrived to try the faith and fortitude of Man through me, his type and symbol. And this thought became an obsession; so that against the clamoring voices of despair I muttered crazily, «I will, I will!» So by the grace of madness I attained the summit.

There, like one who'd passed through ordeal or great sickness, lean and holy, I lay back on the grass. And past my eyes, wide open to the sky, the low clouds moved. Smoothly they moved and silently. It was so quiet there, so high and peaceful!

Then presently I got up. I shouldered my pack that now seemed light, and descended the other side to the lake. And looking back from there along the shore I saw that by climbing the mountain I had gained a hundred yards. It seemed a lot. So, setting my Primus in the shelter of a rock, I made a meal of soup and hard-bread.

I had not continued far, after this refreshment, before I came to the main tributary of the lake, a stream swollen like every other to a formidable size. It now occurred to me that I'd do better to abandon the coast route and trust by following the watershed to circumvent the torrents that had proven such obstacles to progress. It meant hard, uphill work; but since, as I had observed, the mountains extended to the coast they had in any event to be crossed.

How long it took to climb that steep ascent I had no way of knowing; it seemed eternity. My route was rough and tortuous. There's an advantage to a pack and tump-line: you're in harness. Your neck and head are rigid, eyes to the ground ahead; your back is bent to an exact angle of equilibrium, held there; you grip your belt or clasp your hands behind you to sustain the load and rest your tired spine. Your legs are free for nothing but to plod. And looking neither behind you nor ahead, unthinking as a tread-mill mule, rhythmic as clock-work, you put the miles and hours step by step behind.

«And this,» I thought—for still I had the hallucination of being Christian—«is how most labor must be done; for all they tell us now-a-days of loving work!»

Well, I have reached the top and turned; and looking backward wondered how I'd ever come so far. I've made myself some tea and rested a few minutes; but it is cold up here! I go on cheerfully until a chain of lakes confronts me. Now that's been passed.

And I stand in this dreary place wondering what's next, and where. I lay my compass on some moss and, guessing at where I am, take bearings. Good! A broad defile between steep rocks shall be my road. It is a gentle upward slope that soon trends downward. As if I were passing the gateway to my journey's end I hurry through. And there, as far as I can see through gathering gloom and falling rain, the land trends downward; I have crossed the watershed.

Now for a cup of broth, a moment's rest! I feel new-born. «I'll never stop,» I cry as I start running on my way again.

Then suddenly, I've hardly gone two hundred yards, I falter; I'm stumbling, and an incredible weariness comes over me.

There's a projecting shelf of rock that offers shelter. I reach it and let my load fall to the ground. I am utterly tired. It is near midnight, judging by the darkness. Here I shall sleep.

SOME day a learned member of the great Expedition for Historical and Anthropological Researches in Greenland, wandering inquisitively about the highlands of Narsak Peninsula, will come upon such an example of ancient and primitive house construction as must convince him not only of the earlier existence in that region of a cave- or cliff-dwelling race but of the relatively high development of that race as displayed in the execution of its stone work. And what intelligent economy of means to have so used the natural ledges that by the building of one little piece of wall a three walled house roofed by the overhanging ledge had been contrived! There in the decaying moss that so deeply litters the shelf of rock that formed the floor he may discern that they were above all a pleasure-loving race, fond of the comfort of soft beds, of nuptial happiness and sleep. And yet how small must they have been, those mountain men, to have inhabited so cramped a place, so narrow between floor and ceiling as to preclude the entrance even of a well-filled belly! Yes, they were poor and starved, the comfort-loving stone age men, here driven to these barren hills by the more warlike natives of the coast, subsisting here on God knows what! A hardy race!

Oh, he will never know, this scientist, *how* pleasure loving, how possessed by dreams of fireside and food and nuptial ecstasy he was who built that house; how he evoked these flaming dreams against the wet and cold that tortured him through one long, sleepless, miserable midnight hour to drive him, haggard for need of rest, to leave his bed to leap and dance and beat his arms and scream a song out in the darkness and the pouring rain.

Strange things keep happening in the wilderness: is even God aware of them?

AT LAST I could stand it no longer. I forsook my miserable bed, lighted my Primus, made some soup; ate it. I packed my sack and, lifting the soaking thing, dropped the broad tump-line band on to my forehead. Harnessed again!—and the gray light of that near midnight morning showed the way.

Later: For a long time I have been putting my left foot ahead of my right and my right foot ahead of my left; and sometimes it has been uphill and sometimes down; and I've seen grassland and bog, and shale and slippery ledge, and little streams successively glide slowly by beneath my feet. And always the gleam of the lake at my left hand has been my guide.

At last I've come to where that ends. So, resting, I look backward and see how very far I've come. And I look ahead and see that the land drops steeply off, and that there quite far below me lies another lake enclosed by hills. And midway on that lake's far shore, rising abruptly from the water, is a small, steep mountain higher than where I stand. And right and left of that, beyond the lower hills, the ocean!

But Narsak? I turn and climb the last spur of the nearer mountain range. The rain clouds that had hung so low part at my coming and disperse; the sun breaks through—at last, so warm and beautiful! Up, up!

Then suddenly a whole new world of land and sea rises to meet me as I cross the ridge: far snowy peaks and dazzling glimpses of the inland ice, mountains and headlands, islands, bays and inlets; and the ocean—blue and calm. Greenland! Oh God, how beautiful the world can be!

IT WAS again some hours later when having found my bearings from the mountain top I neared the sea. The way had been winding and difficult and there had been wet lands and streams to cross; I was dead tired. But the morning was so beautiful, the sun so warm, the whole scene so enchanting as a place to pitch a tent and settle down to live in for a time, that fatigue as a reason for stopping seemed somehow inappropriate and out of tune. I knew my whereabouts exactly and that my journey's goal, if Narsak, could not lie far away. Why every hilltop promised to disclose it! and as balm for successive disappointments there was each time a farther hill to climb.

Once, having crossed a stream, I sat down in the soft grass bordering it and thought, «Here in the sunlight I'll spread out my things to dry; and here I'll go to sleep.» But when I had bathed my feet, and sat sunning myself a bit, and eaten some chocolate, up I got, shouldered my pack and tramped along. And, as before, I thought, «Just one more hill before I quit!»

So firmly may a stubborn notion grip us, soul and body, that I might have continued that onward movement which is called walking until I had either dropped from exhaustion or circumnavigated the globe but that upon reaching a certain «one more last» ridge, and pausing there to rest, I saw far out on the calm surface of the ocean a little, scarcely moving, speck.

All things in nature seemed to have united there, that morning after days of storm, to achieve tranquillity so perfect that one might say that there was neither sound nor movement beyond the sound and movement of the sunlight. When suddenly that utter silence was shattered by a prolonged, wild, screaming yodel. It filled the valleys, leaped the hills and beat against the mountain faces; its echoes following the scream rolled to the sea, tumbling in prolonged, disordered tumult over its calm plain. And I stood on a pinnacle of rock waving my arms like a madman.

A Greenlander sat in his kayak fishing lazily for cod. The ocean was so still that day, the sun so warm, that all were contented—the cod contented not to eat, and the fisherman too satisfied to care. He even may have slept, the fisherman, so hypnotic on such a day may the rhythm of jigging with a hand-line be. And little did he think that he would hear so soon a sound so startling as a yodel from the wilderness.

He not only heard the sound—to his amazement, fright or, possibly, delight—but he looked up and saw, far off on land, clear cut against the sky, that frantically waving figure, me. So, while the figure came bounding over the landscape toward him, he drew in his hand-line, took up his paddle and turned his craft in timid curiosity to land.

AND here, on the very threshold of a new and great experience, the meeting in a solitary place of men not only
strangers by a social fact but by ten thousand years of
race environment; the meeting of one descended of the
race of the *Mayflower*, of William the Conqueror, Charlemagne,
Brian Boru, etc., and of the culture of Calvin Coolidge, Warren
G. Harding, Dr. Crane, Lincoln, Melville, Goethe, Casanova,
Mother Goose, Caesar and Jesus, Jupiter, Buddha, God, of one
distilled in soul and mind of the fermented mash of all the wit
and wisdom, beauty and virtue, culture and elegance of all the
past, of a Christian Gentleman and Scholar with—God, the
drama of it!—a stone-age man! Here on that threshold—is it to
be wondered at?—I pause.

Earnestly I plead for that attention to the matter of my record which is accorded a wise traveler and competent observer. And yet that I must plead for that may well reveal that I am but too conscious of being without those recognized emoluments of scholarship—titles, degrees, connections and solemn purpose—that lend unquestioned authority to those who have them. It has occurred to me, in searching about for self justification, that despite the high pretentions of the industrious and learned skull measurers and wit weighers of science—biologists, morphologists, tectologists, psychologists, et al—of those who, armed with charts and tables, move to attack the wonder and the mystery of the living, a mere, quite sensitive and well intentioned mortal, I, with no equipment beyond that intuition and common sense which serves most men so well to mix, maintain themselves and mate in life, may hit as near the mark in human things as if I were at least a Ph.D. of Heidelberg.

RUNNING, jumping, stumbling, slipping, running on again I reach the shore. I stand on the rocks of a small promontory, ten feet above the water and look down at the Greenlander in his kayak. And the Greenlander looks up at me. I am a tattered, dirty, haggard and unshaven creature. The Greenlander is dressed in a spotless white anarak, a hooded shirt. He is a dusky man and his brown skin glistens in the sun like polished bronze. His features are oriental: broad cheek bones, small nose, large full mouth and small, black, lustrous eyes. We exchange greetings, seriously, and proceed to conversation.

The fact that he spoke only Eskimo and I spoke none, that speaking no common tongue we fell back upon prelingual callis-

thenics, is—apart from the evolutionary significance of the univer-
sality of look and gesture—of no importance. I told him my story.
I told of how we had sailed in a small boat from America, had
come to Greenland, anchored in the fiord, been wrecked. How
for almost thirty-six hours I had been walking over the mountains. How tired I was. I told it with all the drama of which I was
capable; a great deal. I employed pathos and humor. At my
pathos he looked compassionate; at my humor he smiled—
beautifully. «Oh brother,» I thought, «how just alike we are! But
you are a rich man and I am a poor beach-comber. You're clean
and neat and I am disgusting. You're in your native land, a citi-
zen, at home; and I'm a homeless alien from God knows where!
And while my clumsy hulk of a boat lies smashed up on the rocks
and sunk, you sit there floating in as trim and beautiful a craft as
ever man contrived!» And I knew then—if never I had known it
before—that all that we call civilization, all the taming ennobling,
refining forces of art, science, religion, romance, morals, is an
achievement of no more than an environment into which immu-
tably in endless line man's stone-age babies will be born.

«There is a settlement a little farther on along the shore,» said
the Greenlander. «There's a man there who speaks Danish. You
go by land and I'll go around in my boat and meet you there.»

And as he turned to paddle off I wearily lifted up my pack and
shouldered it.

There was a little inlet of the sea where we had stood convers-
ing, and I had to return a short way inland to pass it. The Greenlander must have turned his head to watch me; he saw how heavily
I trudged along. In a moment he appeared beside me again; passed
me. At the head of the inlet he got out of his kayak, lifted it

dexterously from the water and placed it carefully on land. He came to meet me.

We shook hands. He took the heavy pack from my shoulders and put it on his.

«Have a cigarette,» I said.

Smoking together like old friends we set off at a nimble pace for Narsak.

THEY came running from all directions—bright colored, nimble little figures, men and women, boys and girls and crowds of little children. They poured out of the houses and popped out of the earth. And they all came together, formed a crowd and ran along our way to meet us.

In the midst of all the little folk, running with the rest, was a large man like a giant. He had a round, jolly face, a blond mustache, one gold earring and wooden shoes. Here I thought, is a Dane if ever there was one. We met, shook hands; and I proceeded to tell them all the story of my life.

Everyone found it diverting. Well they might! I pointed far to the south-westward over the sea and said, «America.» And that was understood. I cupped my hands to represent a boat. I

blew on them and rolled them about to show the wind and sea.
I made us enter Karajak Fiord and anchor there. And then, burst-
ing my lungs, I gave a picture of the storm and wreck. The big
man understood. «Come along,» he said in what I assumed to be
Danish. And I went with him to the finest house in the village, his
house. For he was the trader.

He took paper and pen and ink and laboriously transcribed
my story in a letter to the Governor at Godthaab. The story, here
translated, read:

«*Dear Mr. Manager and Sheriff Ch. Simony, K. D.
They came American overland from Karajak on their
boat or ship it sinked with two men. Please be so kind
come, and say to him about, I cannot spoke with him.
Many happy returns,
You and Mrs.   Yours affection.
Thorn Holm.*»

He blotted the letter, sealed it; and ran out with it in his hand.
He gave it to the swiftest kayaker in the village to carry to
Godthaab. Then beaming all over he returned to me. «Make
yourself at home!» he said.

His wife was a Greenland woman prematurely old; wrinkled
and bowed. Their daughter was tall, lithe, dark and very beautiful. They were dressed in that most becoming costume of the
Greenland women—brightly embroidered sealskin shorts, tall
sealskin boots, and a gay colored calico shirt.

I would wash and shave. They brought me hot water and soap
and a Gillette razor, waiting upon me with such sweet grace that

suddenly I realized my loneliness. So when I had made myself clean I went with the trader to the store and, taking off all my clothes, dressed myself anew in the rough, clean garments I could purchase there. Then, feeling quite refreshed and splendid, I went sauntering about the settlement hoping that the girls would fall in love with me. But whether I looked too old or too jaded or too plain or downright foolish, none of them, so far as I know, did. And I had at last to content myself with sitting on a knoll that overlooked the girls and boys, the settlement and the sea, lamenting that I was of none of it a part.

NOW although I am descended, as I may have explained, from Charlemagne, I am continually embarrassed, here, there and everywhere, by discovering poor relatives whose kinship is revealed to me, unfortunately, by our common disgustingness. To avoid incriminating myself by such confessions as might prove my point, I may refer to certain investigations in the field of human behavior conducted by a scientific-minded friend of mine.

This friend occupied an apartment that overlooked a considerable area of the residential section of central Manhattan. From blocks and miles away he was confronted by the front and back façades of tenements, hotels, apartment houses and private dwellings—all packed and swarming with the genus Man. It occurred to him—actuated by only the highest motives—to set up a powerful telescope in one of his windows; and at night, when it is the habit of human kind to retire to the privacy of the bedroom, boudoir and bath, to bring the telescope to bear on such as left their blinds undrawn that he might observe and study how men unobserved may act.

In charges as serious as these I am about to prefer, I lay aside the important, accumulated evidential data of my friend in favor of those things which I myself one night was privileged to see. And yet I may not, even upon the authority of my own first hand observation so far violate the conventions of good taste as to more than suggest the kinds of goings-on that were disclosed to me. Let me rather say—for my whole discussion is directed toward this end—that there's no little filthy, dirty trick of the notoriously dirty Eskimos that's not in kind the practice of our noble Aryan race. Accept this dictum on authority of Peeping Tom.

I would not, however, appear as an advocate of unsecret sin. Let us rather accord it that indulgence which the vice of drinking enjoys, and continue upon the secret enjoyment of our eternal bestiality without the strain of imagining that we're any better than we are.

So—strolling about among the turf houses of the Greenlanders, seeing what I may of how they live, disgusted a little, envious a lot, staring and stared at, laughing and laughed at, charmed by the industry and indolence and general gaiety of all, strolling about or posing on a knoll to contemplate on life and love and dirt and happiness, commiserating me—the hours slip by. Meanwhile what's happening?

TWENTY-TWO Greenlanders are paddling like mad toward Karajak Fiord. There, hard at work salvaging after
ten hours of sleep, are the shipwrecked men. At low
tide they fish things out of the boat; at high tide carry
them to camp. Then come the Greenlanders and a note from me.
A feast to celebrate it! And the crowd, gathered around a blazing
fire, guzzles coffee and hardbread.

Another Greenlander paddles swiftly northward toward God-
thaab. Arrived there, he hurries to the house of the Colony
Manager, Simony, and delivers his letter. «What!» cries Simony,
«Cramer's airplane lost in Karajak Fiord? And two men drowned?»
He sends for the doctor. «Come on, Doctor! they may be saved!»
Both man their separate motor boats and start, full speed.

Along comes the Governor of South Greenland returning from an expedition. They hail his boat and cry the news across. Three boats proceed full speed for Narsak.

I have just finished my dinner at the trader's house; it was a good dinner. And we drank schnapps and beer. Now we sit sipping brandy and smoking large cigars; and we're convivial and happy. So when all at once the squadron of governmental craft comes steaming into the harbor I run to meet them waving the banners of felicity.

The officials stare. «Strange fellow to be laughing—with his comrades dead!»

They land.

The Governor, Mr. Oldendov, is an extremely handsome man, in military dress; a polished gentleman; more courtier, one would think, than outpost governor. I little knew!

Mr. Simony; middle aged, inclined to portliness, to sadness, and to such kindness that it beams from his whole presence. You grasp his hand as of an old, dear friend.

The doctor, Börresen. He wears his tongue in his cheek and winks at me as we exchange a solemn greeting.

I tell my story—in English. They all speak it well.

«Good,» says the Governor. «And have you a permit to land in Greenland?»

Permits to live, permits to die! They made me get a permit to leave Newfoundland the time they put me out!

Well—I had it: permit, passport, letter of credit, cash. And all that being settled we embark for Karajak.

W E'RE off for a resurrection; what but a funeral could be worse. Resurrected life, love, hate, bones; things done, lived, finished, better left alone—dragged into being once again. God spare me that!
Let's get this over with—a nasty business.

«We'll float her!» says the Governor, surveying the tall mast of the *Direction* standing from the water. Five hours to slack tide; off goes a motor boat to Narsak for a load of casks.

Twenty-two Greenlanders sit on the rocks batting at mosquitoes. «Come along Greenlanders to a party!» And they come scrambling to the camp, all grinning and laughing.

There are *Direction's* stores spread out; peas, beans, rice, coffee, tea, corn meal, oat meal, flour, butter, sacks and tins and odds and ends of everything: like kids they scramble for them as we toss them out. «This is for you and this for us. For you, for us; for you, for you, for you—for us.» So it goes on until every man has a bigger pile than he can possibly get into his kayak. And then we come to all that was saved from the toys that we had brought for them—a little wooden toot-horn. They almost fight for it. Then the lucky one, emerging, runs a few steps off and toots it. It makes a funny, feeble, little squawky sound—and they all roar with delight.

So I get out my silver flute and play to them. I play *«Ach du lieber Augustin»* and they all, twenty-two Greenlanders in Karajak Fiord, join in the chorus. And then I yodel to them: that's immense.

Meanwhile the hours pass, the tide falls, and the motor boat, loaded with empty casks, comes chugging back again. *Direction's* deck has now emerged above the water.

«Fill her up with casks,» orders the Governor.

They stuff them down the forward hatch and down the main companionway, one after another till the gutted hold is full. They batten and lash them down. All ready: and now wait, wait for the tide. And the tide creeps slowly up.

Then they attach a bow line and a stern line and a mast head line; and with a motor boat to each begin to pull. They tug and strain, and nothing moves; and the green water is churned white. So once again, and once again. And they rock her by the mast head. And suddenly she moves. All boats full speed ahead! And she begins to slip: keep pulling, everybody! Then almost with a sigh—«Ah, well, if I must live again!»—*Direction*, letting go her hold on death, slides off the ledge—and *floats!*

WE TOWED her to Godthaab, a battered derelict just floating with her deck awash. We moored her near the shore and waited till near midnight for the tide. They beached her then.

Slowly the streaming hulk emerged and climbed the slip; slowly she leaned to port, to rest at last careened high on the land. And the red sun shone on her all glistening wet; and from her opened seams water like blood drops trickled out. There, lying with her lacerated flank to heaven, open to sun and rain and snow, and nesting birds—if any fancy her—we leave *Direction*.

LII

III

IT IS but an hour or two before midnight and I am sitting on a hill above the little settlement of Godthaab. The sun has nearly set and the red beauty of its light is on the land.

I look over the rolling grassy hills of the foreground, at the stark mountains towering at my back; I look over the calm fiord toward far off peaks clear cut against the glowing sky. It is a breathless evening, breathless! And so profoundly beautiful that it is hard to bear alone. And from the settlement comes laughter and the dance music of the accordion.

So I descend to the village and go to the carpenter-shop where the dance is being held. Crowds of young Greenlanders are there; the place is packed. The girls dressed in their finest stand all in a row. They wear bright colored worsted caps, broad bead-work collars over their shoulders, bright colored waists, silk sashes, sealskin shorts, and vermilion boots topped above the knee with a black dogskin band and an embroidered linen cuff. I choose a girl and cross the floor to her. She laughs and yields herself. We put our arms around each other, both arms; and we dance. Here is the music that we dance to:

Four steps forward, four steps back; turn, turn, turn, turn. And oh, how sweetly she dances! We hold each other tight; and she is strong and lithe and young and very beautiful—as Greenland girls can be. And suddenly how dear to me she is! I want to say so to her—and I can't. I want to walk out with her, alone, into the hills and lie with her in the grass of a sheltered spot. We'd lie there and look up at the sky. «Think of it,» I'd say, «in the whole world there are only you and me!» And she'd draw closer to me; we'd feel each other's hearts beat. How we would come to love each other! «Never,» I might say, «have I ever loved so much before!»

But at last the dance came to an end and I had said nothing; for how could I? And presently I went disconsolately home.

I went home and I went to bed. But it was still twilight and through the open window as I lay not sleeping I heard the laughing voices of lovers.

«What rubbish!» I thought. «Along will come some sailor and pinch her thighs; and off to the hills they'll go.»

And, pulling the feather bed about my eyes and ears, as though enveloped in a spurious midnight of my unbelief, at last I slept.

So to maintain some shred of pride against the humiliation of our inaptitude in love have we contrived the lie that romance is a special perquisite of cultured man!

«THERE was once a sealer whose wife was so beautiful that where she was the wind forgot to blow; therefore the sea was always calm before her dwelling. When her husband returned from seal hunting and saw the merest little ripple on the sea then he knew that his wife was in the tent. When, however, his wife was out of doors—then, no matter how the wind blew elsewhere, there where she was, the sea was like a mirror.

«One day her husband was away as usual. He paddled to a great distance and didn't return to his home until evening. He saw great waves beating on the shore and he knew at once that his wife was not there. He landed and entered the tent; it was empty but for some of her clothes. He didn't know where she had gone. So he took down the tent, put his kayak into the water and paddled along the coast. When he had traveled some distance he came to a tent out of which presently there came a man, an extraordinarily large man, whose long hair was bound into a knot at the nape of his neck.

«He called to this man, enquiring if a boat had passed that way.

«And the big man answered:

«'Yesterday a boat passed coming from the south.

«Then the husband asked:

«'Can I get someone here to help me paddle?'

«The big man answered that he could get him an orphan boy; and he asked him meanwhile to come ashore and eat a dainty mess of sauerkraut and putrid liver. The sealer went into the man's house, hastily partook of the food, and immediately went upon his way again, accompanied by the orphan.»

Again he comes to a tent where lives a big man; and everything happens as before. And again he is upon his way. The story continues:

«They paddled and paddled along the coast until they came near to a dwelling place where the water in the vicinity of the tent was quite calm, though here and there the sea was agitated. Then he knew that his wife was in that place; but the movement of the sea revealed that she was not as beautiful as before, because she was unhappy.»

B
UT, now that love has entered the narrative, let us before proceeding dispose in one spiteful chapter of that concentrated object of my hate, the mate, and pay his personality the grateful tribute not of having so much merited my loathing as of having served to foster in me such a need to love that, freed at last of his infuriating presence, the sun of my good nature shone as from a cloudless sky on everything. Love would lack poignancy but for its corollary, hate.

The mate was, fortunately, so naïvely unconscious of his own ungraciousness that the seeds of his early departure from Greenland were sown in prompt discourtesies toward those who were to be his hosts. It was a social error, surely, on that first long trip from Karajak to Godthaab, to have parked his bulk full length on the settee of the Governor's cabin, to sleep there while the tired Governor sat nodding on a soap box.

Seventy-eight hours after the morning of the wreck I lay down in the doctor's house at last for the first time to sleep. I closed my eyes and the sweetness of oblivion descended over me. Suddenly there was a loud knocking on the door. The ex-mate entered. «Say,» said he, «where in Hell did you put the cigarettes?» The cigarettes were in the storehouse; I got them out. Of all that had been saved only six cartons were dry. The mate went off with them: exeunt cigarettes. At midnight, eight hours later, I was free at last to sleep.

Greenland is a closed country. It is administered by the Danes with the single purpose—strange in this age of exploitation—of preserving to the natives the free enjoyment of their land, forever. And while the instruction of the Greenlanders in the ways of modern civilization and the doctrines of St. Paul is deemed essential to the achievement of their ruler's Christian purpose, so carefully has their diet of enlightenment been weighed that the intrusion of irresponsible foreigners, even of Danes, is not tolerated. The difficulties of procuring the permission of the Danish Greenland Department to visit Greenland are serious and many. Senseless as these had seemed to me when I applied to be allowed to go there, I came at last to view my permit as an honor and a responsibility. So, finding myself now with two companions, thrown upon the hospitality of the colony, I chose to consider the slothfulness and bad manners of the mate as entitling him to nothing but the government's tactful suggestion that he leave by the first steamer. He did. And the only sorrow I felt at the leave-taking was that the skipper, as fine and good and brave a boy as ever walked or sailed, went too.

P RELIMINARY to that sailing was the inquiry by the High Court in Admiralty of Greenland into the circumstances of the wreck. It was presided over by the Governor in his capacity of Chief Magistrate; and I may record that the splendor of his appearance on that occasion in the regalia of his office was visually expressive of his distinguished administrative talent.

I introduce some portions of the finding of that court less for the interest of their factual content than for the chaim of the translation which a daughter of Knud Rasmussen has made for me. It follows:

Transcription of the law for South-Greenland.
In the year 1929—Saturday the 20th of July 1 o'clock began the

*meeting in Godthaab by the Ordinary Judge Knud Oldendov, the
Provincial Judge C Simony and the assistant from the Greenland-
Direction L. Hagesen, both from Godthaab, as improvement witness,
for the Justice interpreter the assisten from the fox-breeding—V. S.
Lund.*

*The Judge observed that he had been with the wrecking place and
together with the Colony-Director, both of them tried to help. He could
certify that the weather on the wrecking-day had been extraordinary
bad.*

*The Witness; Arthur Samuel Allen—Born 8 May 1907—Brook-
lyn-Massachussets—who was the owner of the boat. He exposed:*

The Journal of the DIRECTION *cutter, summer 1929. And the
Navigation-Law says that he is the captain of the boat.*

*He explained that the boat was insured but he did not know the
insure-price. His Father has insured it, and he did'nt know the insur-
ance-office. He told that they only put one anchor out when the boat
went in drift at 10.30 o'clock 15 July. The second anchor at 11
o'clock after having driven half an hour cross the bay. This second
anchor were putting out after they been driven the half way from the
originally anker-place to the wrecking-place. Those two ankers could
not hold the boat, then he tried to put the sail on, but the storm made
it impossible. After which he tried the 3 anker but it miscarryed—and
the boat knock.*

*The boat was flowing nearly one hour after the wrecking—and
then it went down. On that time it was high-water.*

*It was impossible to try to bring the boat right. All people on board
have lost a great deal of their personal propriety. A. S. Allen think
he have lost about 50 dollars.*

The price of the boat was about 8,000 dollars. He can have the boat

repaired on the place here and get permission to come back next sum-
mer and fetch it. He can—from his home—pay a sum of money for
the necessary expenses.

He mean that the best thing to do is to get the necessary reparation
materials from Denmark after the originally draught of the boat. He
will take care of the draught and try to get it via Copenhagen as soon
as he can. He want permission to come back next summer to fetch the
boat but have to apply ones self to the government of Denmark.
Proclaimed   *Admitted*

The Witness; Rockwell Kent—Born 21-Jun-1882 Cook on board
and navigator—but ex professo painter and author and the proper
leader of the expedition. He has nothing to append to the report of
Allans. It is correct exactness and detailed. He has lost for about 300
dollars provisions. Of his personal properties was two camera with
films (for about 340 dollars) one barometer (25 dollars) a gold watch
(125 dollars) All together about 800–1,000 dollars.

R.K. wants to be «representeret» in the assurance and eventuelt
name the 300 dollars. If it should come to disbursement. That ques-
tion will be accound in America. At last he want to express his thank-
fullness and admiration for the «resolute» quickly work and good
help to save the boat.
Proclaimed   *Admitted*

The Witness; Cupid—Born 21 Jan 1907—Chicago—Student and
Journalist. on board steersman; he have nothing to say (append)—
he only want to mark that he has never thought a storm could have
such a strength degree. He has only lost for about 50 dollars.
Proclaimed   *Admitted*

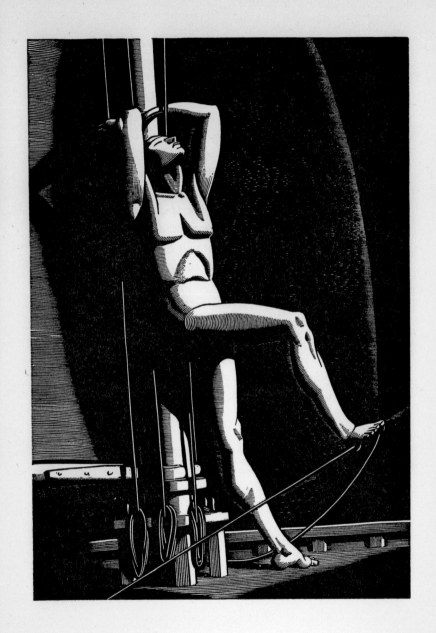

THE loss of some hundreds of dollars worth of «personal propriety,» of which the Admiralty Court took cognizance, contributed no doubt to that high liberation of the spirit which the wilderness invited. Only those men who have through shipwreck, drunkenness or chance achieved such a loss have tasted freedom; and in a world inclined to tame the wilderness and eliminate the hazards from experience we may well cling to the ancient, high born, salutary privilege of man— of getting, sometimes, drunk.

See me then liberated by the blessedness of disaster from the confinement of a boat, shorn of property, stripped of clothes, wandering, an unknown alien beach-comber, in a generous land. And if these pages fail to glow with the riotous adventure of bloodshed and unbridled lust suspect them less of concealing what occurred than of reflecting the profounder truth that with all freedom in the world to carry on we'd most of us by nature act quite decently.

NOW after I had been some days in Godthaab I came to know that certain articles and supplies which, at the time of the general dispersal of salvaged goods at Karajak, I had retained for my own use were somehow now in the possession of the natives of Narsak. So, to enquire into that matter, as well as to settle certain charges which I had incurred at the time of the wreck, I accompanied Manager Simony on a visit there. Together we conferred with the trader, Holm.

«They say,» began Holm, «that you should pay them for the labor they performed at the wreck.» At that we all laughed for it was well known that we had given them veritable riches in goods.

«Very well,» I said. «And suppose I pay them a kroner each?»

«That is most generous,» said the trader.

And I handed across twenty-two kroner.

«The man whom you first met,» continued the tiader, «and who carried your pack into Narsak says that you promised to pay him.»

Now I had singled him out, at the giving away, to receive all kinds of special gifts from me. I had thought him amply rewarded. But gifts are one thing and pay according to contract is another, I saw the point; it was a good one. Five kroner for him. Eleaser Poolsen, so he was named, was delighted.

I wanted desperately to procure a pair of native sealskin boots, for I was still going about in my heavy rubber boots, and had no shoes. But even the natives find it hard to keep supplied with footwear; sealskins are scarce. My want was told to Eleaser. He went out. Presently, he returned with a fine new pair of boots that his wife had just finished for him. He gave them to me and would accept no pay.

Then the trader sent for the chief men of the settlement and told them how it was known that the Greenlanders had in their houses certain things which had not been given to them.

«Everything,» said the head-man, «that they have that came from the wreck shall be produced.»

And in a few minutes from all the houses came people laden with our late goods and chattels. They spread them out in a long line on the grass. When all was there I began and chose from the aggregate those things which I now needed. But these I divided into two piles; one pile of things that had not been given to them, and the other of things which had been given but which I now wanted back.

«The first,» I said, «are mine. The others, having been given to you are yours. I offer to buy them.»

For every article I then named a price. This was translated to a head-man and he passed it on to his constituent, the owner. My offers met with their approval. I paid the money; and amid general merriment the large remainder of goods was carried back to the houses.

So with the true and simple logic of children do they now reason. But some day, as the world goes, they'll have—God help them—law and politics. And they'll learn that taking things is stealing, and that gifts received entail an obligation.

SERMALIK is Greenlandish for glacier-bay; the name is borne by many Greenland fiords. On the shore of that Sermalik Fiord which penetrates the wild foreland forty-five miles south of Godthaab is pitched my tent; here I am living for a week. Hereabouts I paint, carrying my canvases over the hills or rowing to more distant places in my boat.

At the head of the fiord appears the inland ice; and my eyes may follow the inclined plane of the glacier up from where its blue cliffs are reflected in the water to the glistening mountain-high horizon of that limitless plateau of ice which, but for the narrow ice-free foreland on the sea, would be all Greenland. On every hand are mountains of Archean rock, rounded or rising sheer to jagged ridges or to peaks capped with perpetual ice.

Confronting my camping site from across the fiord is a smaller mountain called by the Greenlanders a name which means «like a mountain.» Somehow I have come to be always looking at it. And the morning light and evening and the low sun at noon, reveal as though from many sides the fair proportions of its mountain architecture. So like a mountain does it look at last to me that had I been God I would, I know, have made no other.

Not until darkness is at hand do I prepare my supper, for even these long days are far too short for all their beauty. Suddenly—it is now dark—a prolonged, high-pitched barking breaks the stillness; turning my eyes to the sound I see, silhouetted against the sky on the dark ridge of the hillside, a little blue fox. He sticks his sharp nose up at Heaven and for an hour howls away.

ONE day as I sat at work I heard a gunshot and, looking up, saw two kayaks and an umiak or women's boat filled with people approaching my camp from the direction of the mouth of the fiord. A few minutes brought them close to shore where I had gone to greet them. I invited them all up to the tent, and tentwards, after shaking hands all around, we went. It was a rainy afternoon so we all gathered under the canvas; and the guests—three men, four women and several children—squatted about expectantly while the kettle came to boil. In little time we were all drinking hot coffee with lots of sugar in it and eating rye bread spread extremely thick with butter.

There was plenty of laughter and in that I joined; but of the conversation I could understand no word. We may assume it to have been of the desultory order of tea-party conversations in general. Presently, the repast having been finished, the guests arose, thanked me cordially and took their departure. They presented me with a large, dead sea gull for my dinner.

Two men got into their kayaks and the third enthroned himself on top of the household goods in the stern of the umiak; the women, as usual, manned the oars. We waved to each other from time to time until the boats passed out of sight behind a bend in the fiord.

These Greenlanders came undoubtedly from one of the remoter settlements. They were possibly as «primitive» as any in the colony. I have described the meeting with them in all its eventfulness as a picture, but for the nature of the food dispensed, of what a tea-party may have been in stone age days. Life normally must always have been uneventful!

BUT far from uneventful were these shores five hundred years ago; the century of the discovery of the new world by Columbus witnessed the decline and miserable end of the ancient and once thriving new world settlement of Greenland. And it is possible that in the very hour that the *Santa Maria's* mast-head watch cried out, «Land Ho!» Ungortok, the last Viking where ten thousand once had lived, fell, as the Greenland legend tells, under «a magic arrow, made of the extremest cross-piece of a barren woman's hip-bone. Thus,» says the legend, «died the last of the old Kablunaks.»

But even now the ruins of their buildings may be seen; churches —some with their four walls standing to the very gable peak, dwellings in ruin, barns, store houses, sheep enclosures; and the fields that once were cultivated still show more flowers and verdure than the surrounding moor.

Far from the ocean, at the heads of the several branches of Ameralik and Godthaab Fiords, lie the farm ruins of the old «Western Settlement» of the sagas. And at the head of Ujaragssuit Fiord, on a sloping plateau that ends in a steep bank at the water's edge, deep in a luxuriant copse, stand the four walls of what must once have been a church. It was a small structure built of unhewn stones; but so substantially and well were those walls built that, but for the minor depredations of the Eskimos, they stand today as when they first were raised. Yet it is difficult, even at the side of that reminder of the past, to see that wilderness as once a prosperous and cultivated country-side, to recall to it in thought the blond descendants of the race of Erik—farmers, tilling their fields, tending their flocks; living and loving here as they had done in Iceland; calling this place home. Yet so it once had been.

And trading ships came every year from Norway bringing them grain to brew their ale, and wood; conveying home such Greenland products as ivory and oil. They brought the latest news of kings and kin; of fashions; and now and then they brought a Bishop consecrated by the Pope in Rome.

Then came those troubled times abroad when through recurrent pestilence and war Greenland was, first—neglected, then—forgotten. And upon that began the long, slow course of their starvation. The misery of that the graves at Herjolfnes have now revealed to us.

Of the killing in South Greenland of the last man, as it is remembered in Eskimo tradition, we have already told. But the beginning of that end is laid in Ujaragssuit Fiord.

In the early years of the settlements the Norsemen and the Eskimos lived at peace with one another; and all was well. But at last there arose a quarrel over a woman. Now the Eskimos were in summer camp on Ujaragssuit Fiord. One day, while the men were absent from the tent-place on a reindeer hunt, the Norsemen attacked the women, killing all but one.

Determined on revenge the Eskimos built an umiak, covering it with beautiful white skins and a few dark ones, so that it might resemble floating ice. And it was so contrived that, filled with men, it could float turned over on one side while the men, concealed within it, could observe all that went on. Seen from the land it really did resemble a little, dirty piece of calf ice, as its surface was alternately shining and dusky.

Meanwhile the Norsemen had fled for safety to Ameragdla Fiord where, united with others of their race, they trusted to repel the impending assault of the Eskimos.

The umiak of the attackers came drifting into Ameragdla Fiord before a westerly breeze; it neared the farm at Kilarsarfik. The men hidden within the boat caught glimpses of the Norsemen going in and out of the dwelling house. They were keeping watch across the fiord. Then one of the Norsemen called out so loudly that it could be heard on the water; «It's not a boat, but only a piece of ice.» At that all of them went back into their dwelling.

The Eskimos now landed. They crept up to the house and stealthily piled fuel all about it and in the passage-way of the entrance. Then, with fire they had brought with them, they set it aflame. Some of the Norsemen perished by burning; others were killed with arrows. A certain man named Big Olav, happening to be returning at that very time from catching seals (he was the only Norseman of them all with enough courage left him to go hunting every day) was also killed.

But the Norse chieftain, whom the Eskimos called Ungertok, taking his young son in his arms, leapt through a window and escaped. And it was he who was at last to perish as the last survivor of the Eastern Settlement.

But another man, a servant, also got away; he boarded a craft having light sails. And as his pursuers reached the shore behind him they heard him shout, «When it blows gently in the morning at Big-Ameralik, then will come an east wind.» So the east wind came. And as it bore him out of the fiord he was heard to cry out sorrowfully, «Ah, you beautiful wood-clad slopes!»

BUT that was centuries ago. In Greenland the environment of nature dominates; and into the sparse settlements along its rim of shore, into men's thoughts and
moods and lives has entered something of the eternal
peacefulness of the wilderness. It had to be. Man is less entity
than consequence and his being is but a derivation of a less subjective world, a synthesis of what he calls the elements. Man's very
spirit is a sublimation of cosmic energy and worships it as God;
and every faculty to feel, perceive and know serves only to relate
him closer to what is. God is the Father, man his connatural prog-
eny; and thus the elements at work become for man the pattern
for his conduct, the look and feel and sound of them—sunshine
and storm, peace and turmoil, lightning and thunder and the quiet

interludes—the formulae for his poor imitative moods and their expression. But in the wilderness invariably peace predominates; and seeing the quiet uneventfulness of lives lived there, their ordered lawlessness, the loveliness and grace of bearing and of look and smile that it so often breeds and fosters we may indeed «lament what man has made of man» and hold those circumstances of congestion which are called civilization to be less friendly to beauty than opposed to it.

More than two hundred years ago there came a Christian militant, Hans Egede, to Greenland, and brought those heathen folk the Gospel law. And Greenland, its wilderness and wilderness's heathen folk, reached out and gently laid its peaceful spirit upon Egede and all who followed him and lived there. Thus came the natives of Greenland to learn somewhat of the virtues of cleanliness and industry and thrift, and the Christians to become more godly, decent, quiet, honorable, fair than any Christians aggregate I've met with elsewhere in the world. Christ, too, if I remember, sojourned in the wilderness.

SO IT has come to pass that, being now with this third portion of my narrative in Greenland, it is of *quiet* happenings I have to write. No murders, quarrels, no more hazards, shipwrecks, ordeals, no climax of adventure; we have passed those peaks, and enter, as books go, the dreaded region of the anticlimax. «And so,» they tell us, having told of labors ended, «they lived happily forever after»—and are done with it. But how? Are lives so happy as to need no pictures of contentment or shall shipwreck be its own fulfilment—stopping there? For what, I came to think, had I endured the misery of that crossing, and the wreck, the hours of hardship following, but to emerge more fit to feel men's kindliness and to experience contentment in the uneventfulness of daily life as here I found it? So must what happened here concern us less than, with the premise of my happiness and everyone's, those facts of uneventfulness that nourished it.

Always in Godthaab and in every colony, quite isolated as they are, immured from one another by the rugged, fiord-indented intervening wilderness, backed by high mountains and the inland ice, fronting the sea, always one felt that there in that small cluster of houses were gathered all there was of human kind, huddled for need of one another against the terrifying immensity of the earth and sky. America and Europe—even the nearer settlements—seemed far away as lands but dimly known; and it was each time with something of the spirit of the early adventurers that men went out excursioning; and they returned each time leaving the wilderness unmarked.

ONE morning when the sun shone bright as usual, from a cloudless sky, when people were finishing their morning coffee and the Greenland girls were gathering for their carefree stevedoring at the wharf, there emerged simultaneously from the house of the governor and the house of the doctor, governor and doctor and attendants and me all bearing hampers, wraps, guns, canvases, all laden to go voyaging on Godthaab Fiord. We stowed our things, embarked and sailed. *«Farvel!»* we cried. *«Farvel, farvel!»* came out to us across the widening water. As if we were sailing to the world's end, but far gayer, was that leave-taking.

Of Greenland, what a day! How blue the mountains and the sea, golden the sky! the grassy slopes how green—rich green and bright with flowers! What fellowship on board! There in the labyrinthine passages of Godthaab Fiord, tossing the beauty of the world to heaven as laughter, there, singing *«Clementine»* and *«Old Black Jo,»* we drank in amber *Gammle Carlsberg,* *«SKOAL!»* to thee and me and us and everything. Thus carrying on—as fine a tribute surely to the gorgeousness of that today as some more solemn ecstasy—we came late in the afternoon to Korkut Fiord; there pitched our tents. The place became our playground: some explored, some fished for salmon, one made a picture of the scene and then, so hot the day, went swimming. Till late we sat and smoked and chatted; then with the sun still lighting up the peaks, turned in and slept like kids.

Early to rise, and coffee as we sailed along. Stopped at a summer settlement of natives camped in tents; we visited. The doctor looked at a complaining old man's foot and found nothing the matter with it; and he gave castor oil to an old woman who certainly needed it. Then, as though to purge our skins of all contamination from those dirty tents, we stripped and, to the admiration of the natives all, plunged in the sea and swam.

Again, in Pisigsarfik Fiord where natives were encamped beside a salmon stream, we stopped a while, called at the tents and chatted, those who could, with the more talkative. It is a salutary thing, that summer life for Greenlanders. Their winter homes—the older type with earthen walls—lie open meanwhile to the sun and rain. They need a season's sun and rain, and profit by it. How dirty would we be, the cleanest of us, who had to live, not for a week or month or year, but always on and on successively from birth to grave like that!

Here once were farms of Norsemen, and the dense thickets of

birches growing near the shore were evidence of the land's fertility. We struggled through them to a distant hill and looked across a narrow isthmus to where Kangersunck Fiord lay filled with glacial ice. The day was warm, the going hard; returning tired and hot we bathed again in the clear, cool water of the fiord.

And with evening it grew cold and a strong wind came up. Down in the twilight of the fiords we drove along to make Kasertak island for the night. We watched the sun's last rays pass from the mountain peaks, and darkness come. In darkness we made port. There on a narrow shelf of land with the sheer wall of the island's mountain towering above us, feeling out comfortable ground to sleep upon, we pitched our tents.

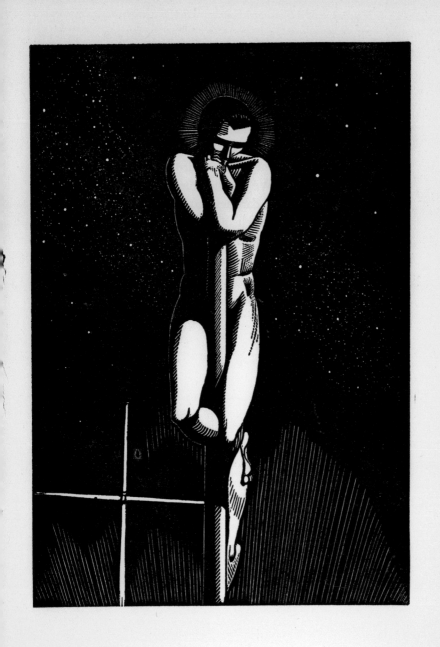

IT WAS the next day, nearly noon, that we bore into Ujar-agssuit Fiord. From far away appeared its ruin standing on the plain. The fiord is shoal and murky with the silt of the glacial stream that enters at its head; we anchored a full quarter mile from where we'd hoped to land. Even our dory grounded several yards from shore. They were no fishermen who once lived here!

I contrived to go alone to the ruin for I felt the premonition of a mood more solemn than I cared to show. And as I worked through the rank underbrush that encumbered the way I found myself avoiding the destruction of the least twig of it and treading stealthily as though there were about the place some spirit of the perished race that once had lived there.

The walls stood eight feet high, half hidden by the brush. Three sides were blind, but in the fourth was a low doorway. I entered. It was heaped with stones where the wall's coping and the gable ends had fallen in.

I climbed the wall and from that eminence looked out over the sunlit, smiling wilderness of fiord and mountains. But so heavily were my thoughts weighted with reflection that seemed almost memory that the very calmness of the scene enhanced as though through mockery its Godforsakenness. If it had only stormed or wept it so had shown some warmth of fellowship for what had once befallen in its midst. «For this oblivion,» I thought, in bitterness, «those exiles left their Iceland farms!» And so there came to mind the grief, not hope, that must have marked their coming here. Yet one man, exiled, stayed.

Gunnar, in Iceland, rode off toward his ship. Down along Markfleet on the way he fell. «He turned with his face up toward the Lithe and the homestead at Lithend, and said—

'Fair is the Lithe; so fair that it has never seemed to me so fair; the cornfields are white to harvest, and the home mead is mown; and now I will ride back home, and not fare abroad at all.'»

So Gunnar did; and there they killed him.

S O, EXCURSIONING and voyaging about, landing to stroll the settlements or climb the neighboring hills, look- ing at everything and listening, I came at last to have been north to Seventy and south to Sixty-thirty. My lingual limi- tation served to sharpen the perceptive faculties and shield me from dependence on such facts as others might have told me. It was, in consequence, what *seemed* to be that made my Greenland world; and such conclusions as I ventured on were reached inversely, from effect to cause. All that *looked* beautiful to me, was good; and if I held the smile of the Eskimo to be evidence of his serenity of soul, the inter-racial courtesy of the Danes to show the virtue of their ruler- ship, and both to prove that life in Greenland's solitudes was good for man my thought at least began where science stops.

How rich in everything was Greenland! Whether **I** sought the wilderness to find in mountain forms the substantive of abstract beauty or to renew through solitude the consciousness of being; or whether, terrified by both, I turned gregarious and needed love or friendship or to rub shoulders in a Greenland dance—all, everything was there. And no more complete with majesty were the mountains, nor limitless the ocean, than human kind seemed what it ought to be.

EVERY day I went off early in the morning into the country, carrying my canvases and paints; and most days I remained there until nightfall. Sometimes I'd travel miles, and it was heavy work. At noon I'd sit in some warm, sheltered spot munching my chocolate and crackers, reflecting upon my happiness or not thinking at all. I'd rest a while or walk about exploring; those were most peaceful, lovely hours.

One day in northern Greenland I had gone farther than usual along the coast, to start my work at last in the midst of a broad, rolling piece of foreland stretching between tall mountain ranges and the sea. It was a clear, brisk day; so, delighting in the warmth of the sun I went at noontime for a stroll.

I climbed a hill and stood there looking over the blue ocean. «Here I am, at land's end,» I thought, «and the ocean is the absolute. Therefore, here by the ocean, one could live forever and desire nothing more.»

Then suddenly, in a depression of the land below me, I saw a tiny moving figure, bright vermilion. And I knew what that was. I forgot the sea and the mountains and the sunshine and the absolute and stood there watching how the little figure crept along. Then, all at once, it stopped. So far apart that they appeared to each other as the tiniest specks on the vast landscape, a woman and a man stood looking at each other. And both knew it. Then, at the very same moment, they moved a little bit; they waved their arms in greeting.

We walked towards each other, sometimes in view, sometimes hidden in the hollows. Our meeting came as though unexpectedly, so near and sudden was our last emergence from the cover. Yet we were not embarrassed. We walked together to a sheltered spot where the sun was warm; there we sat down side by side, and she began to talk to me.

I had little idea of what she said; but by such noddings and shakings of the head as I thought appropriate she came to believe that I understood her words. And soon we were laughing together. We kissed each other, and I made love to her; but she was reluctant. Therefore, it being the drowsy hour of noon, I lay back on the grass. I saw her laughing face shadowed against the blue zenith; she petted me and prattled on. And presently I slept.

How could I know how long! After a time I awoke. I opened my eyes and saw her there, sitting up straight beside me. Her hand rested affectionately on my knee; her eyes were on the horizon of the ocean—but as though not seeing it. And in a low, sweet voice she sang a song. I shall never know what the words of that song were.

They may have been these:

> "I sing this little song
> the worn little song of another,
> and I sing it as my own
> my own dear little song.
> And thus I play
> with this worn song,
> over and over"

For a long time I hid from her that I was awake. At last, as we were parting, she asked me to give her my soiled pocket handkerchief. Oh, if I had only had a thousand new ones for her!

AT NUK in the North Greenland district of Egedesminde lived a certain trader of half native blood. Some errand brought me to his house with Peter Freuchen. The house was substantial and large but as destitute of what to us are homelike furnishings as the house of the most unenlightened native. And yet the trader was a man of worth and had prepared for priesthood.

He was an active man past middle life, and a famed hunter. Being asked his age he answered:

«I can still hunt the seal and put barrels together. What do the years matter?»

He spoke to Peter of a certain mutual friend of theirs and Rasmussen's, an Eskimo. And it was told how he one day started with his dog team on a long journey. After traveling for many hours he came at last to where another's sledge tracks crossed his route. On seeing them he turned about and drove back home. He explained that it had not been his plan that day to cross another's tracks.

While on another journey his road led through a narrow mountain pass. He followed it and soon emerged upon a broad valley. At that he turned back. It was not his plan, he said, to travel that day in a broad valley. His brother, the trader told us, was like that, too.

We laughed, and called them crazy.

«No,» said the trader, «we must not say that he was crazy. He came from Baffin Land. It may be that it is the custom of the people there to act that way.»

The trader had recently seen for the first time the Danish motor ship *Disco* of the Greenland service. «That ship must be,» he told us fervently, «the largest ship in the world.»

Then, to show off, I told him that there were ships six times as long as the *Disco*.

He laughed at that.

«No,» he said, «for so long a ship would bend in the water and could not be steered.»

But at last we convinced him that it was really possible and true; and at that his pride and happiness were gone, for he had no longer seen the biggest ship in the world.

ONE night I walked alone along the road of a North Greenland settlement, back and forth alone from end to end of it. And it was thronged with groups and couples of young men and girls; the air was rippling with the sound of their laughter. Soberly I strode there, looking dignified; no wonder that the Greenland girls all looked at me and laughed! At last I could bear it no longer—neither their laughter nor the way they looked; nor my desires.

I came to the end of the road where it peters out and is lost in the hills. There were two girls just turning back; we all met face to face and all began to laugh. So I came between them and put my arms about their shoulders and began to talk English to them very fast. They answered me in a torrent of Eskimo; and it was so foolish that all at once we were great friends. Then the girls said something to each other; whereat one slipped from my arm and ran away—and two of us stood close together in the growing darkness. She looked down the road and saw that no one was near. We turned and ran off hand in hand toward the hills.

Now there are many eyes hidden in those hills at night; and she was timid. So I took off my white anarak and stuck it under the gray sweater that I wore. Now we were hardly to be seen.

We went very far into the hills, climbing over ledges, leaping pools; she was as agile and as silent as a wild creature. At last we came to a hidden spot carpeted with moss; so shadowed was it by an overhanging cliff that not even the starlight seemed to be there.

Sometimes, some hours when the world is wonderfully beautiful, all at once the universe is hushed and motionless as if to make more poignant that seen beauty. So, as we lay there in the darkness, silent and seeing nothing, it was as if all loveliness was only to be known by touch.

Oh, it was a long time later when we came again, hand in hand, to the road of the settlement. Lamps were still burning in some windows. We paused where the light from one streamed out over the roadway. And by the light she saw that a hole had been torn in her bead collar. She looked at me with deep reproach, and I thought that she would cry.

I tried to show my sympathy. Crumpling some money into a wad I drew it, hidden in my hand, out of my pocket and held it, covered, to her.

But she saw it. She drew away from me, offended. I was ashamed.

Then suddenly I went up to her and took the torn part of her collar in my hand. And with my other hand I passed the money through the hole and gave it to her. She took it, and smiled her forgiveness.

IT IS September and the days grow shorter; I am sailing south. Cold nights and shortened days, southward and— home! And so the revisitation of the places I have known is tinged a little with the melancholy of leave-taking. It is the season of leave-taking in Greenland; fall is at hand and the long, dark months of winter quickly follow.

On many sites in Greenland I have built myself, in fantasy, a home, so beautiful and friendly have they been. Yet in the midst of all of it, even with the very thought of how one could for all his life quite happily live here, the consciousness of elsewhere has crept in and homesickness in flesh and blood stalked through the visionary walls. And all that I had imagined stood exposed as but a reconstruction of such things as were already mine.

I stood at a boat's rail with Christian Simony of Godthaab and we looked over the water upon a towering landscape of bare hills and granite mountains lit into splendor by the setting sun. «How beautiful it is!» I cried impulsively. Then suddenly I remembered his prevailing sadness and the cause of it that everybody knew. And how through all his years in Greenland he had never forgotten the flat meadow lands and the beech forests of Denmark, but more and more yearned to return there. So that at last he bore the look of one whose thoughts are always on some unattainable beyond.

"THERE is a legend of a sealer from Aluk who never left the place where he was born. He loved his dwelling-place so dearly that he was reluctant to go elsewhere to catch seal; but then he never suffered want where he was.

«But this man had a son; and when his understanding awoke he realized that he had never been outside Aluk. When the other men of the dwelling-place went out on hunting expeditions he often wished to go with them, but as he was very fond of his father he never showed it. At times he made attempts to rouse his father's inclination to travel, but the father only answered: 'From the moment that I took land at Aluk, I do not remember ever having left it.'

* 237 *

«But whenever they were left behind alone, and all the young men had departed for strange coasts, the son became silent.

«When midsummer came the father could not sleep in the morning at the hour when the sun rose above the country. It was said that it was because he must see it rise above the sea, while the rays, as it were, splintered against icebergs. This sight moved him so deeply that it was impossible for him to leave his dwelling-place.

«Thus the years passed. But when, because of old age the father was unable to go sealing, and the son had to do it alone, he could no longer resist the temptation to see the world; and so on one fine spring day he said to his father:

«'This time I intend to leave my dwelling-place and to go and look for new things in strange parts.'

«For a long time he waited for his father to reply, but the latter remained silent; and as he did not answer, the son once more tried to conquer his desire to travel. Only later on, when he could no longer hold his thoughts in check, he determined not to let himself be silenced, until his father had acceded to his request.

«Once when he returned from a sealing trip and they sat waiting for the evening to fall upon them he again began to speak to his father:

«'This time it must be; now I want to leave my country and go north and look for new things in strange parts.'

«But the father did not answer. Not until the son once more addressed him did he see that now there was no way out.

«'But then we will not go too far north, and you must promise me that we shall return to our dwelling-place.'

«The son was very happy, and he eagerly set about making his umiak ready for the journey.

«And one morning when the weather was fine they at last started north. And they traveled far, far; and the farther north, the better the son liked the country.

«And they traveled and traveled, and it was the first time that the father had been away from his native place for so long. And the more the summer advanced, the more he saw his country in his thoughts before him. He longed for it so that after a while sleep left him; and in the morning at the time when the sun rose, he could not sleep, for he ever felt impelled to go out in order to see whether the sunrise would be as it was at his native place. But always the mountains blocked the horizon so that it was impossible to see the first peep of the sun.

«At first the old man would not speak about it to his son, but when he could no longer bear his yearning he spoke up, saying:

«'Let us now return; otherwise I shall die with longing!'

«It was hard for the son to return now that the country became more and more beautiful in his sight. And yet he once more shaped his course towards the south, as the words of his father kept sounding in his ears.

«But although they were now on their way home it was as if the father was only getting worse and worse, for he hardly ever slept; and when they awoke in the morning he was walking about outside the tent. They traveled and traveled, and at last they came back to their dwelling-place.

«Quite early on the following morning the son awoke at the sound of his father's voice; and the words he heard were:

«'No wonder that it is hard to leave Aluk! Behold, the great sun when it rises above the sea, and its rays break against the icebergs of the horizon.'

«And he heard the old man repeatedly utter exclamations of joy; and then everything was quiet. He listened for a long while, but as he heard no sound from his father, who was just outside the tent opening, he got up and pulled aside the tent covering. And lo—there lay the old man on the ground with his face turned towards the east. And when the son lifted him up he did not breathe.

«Thus the old sealer once more saw the sun in his native place. His joy was so overwhelming that his heart burst. And the son, who felt guilty of the death of his father, built a grave for him on the top of the mountain, overlooking the view which he had loved while alive.

«And later on it was told that he came to be like his father, nor did he ever leave his dwelling-place, but remained at Aluk until the end of his days.»

TODAY there is to be a christening and tonight the party; and tomorrow I sail from Greenland.

«You shall be grander than I, tonight,» says my dear friend the doctor; for there has always been a controversy between us as to which of us by nature was the more magnificent.

He got out a suit of evening clothes—a little creased, a little worn, spotty perhaps and old, but, oh, how elegant! It fitted me!

We were a little late in starting, for Frk. Holmgaard—our little housekeeper—would have no spot or fleck to show. And when I was all dusted off and clean and finished they put a long overcoat on me and buttoned it to the neck, and we all ran to the party.

I never know how much to say about such personal triumphs as

I thought that was for me that night. It was natural that the distinguished guests, having hitherto known me only in the garb of a beach-comber, should be amazed, dumbfoundered and delighted; and that I, buoyed by my own complacency, elated by the occasion and carried away by that general excitement to which my courtly presence may have contributed, should drink too much. At last, comprehending not one word, and being moved almost to tears by the eloquence of the Governor—because, as he told me, I *couldn't* understand it, I suddenly found myself standing in the middle of the floor with everyone at attention around me. I had announced that I was about to make a speech.

«Oh, little baby,» I began, «poor, tiny, shipwrecked mariner thrown, as I was, helpless and naked on this coast, here at the mercy of strangers, here to be clothed and housed and fed and taught by them, here in the wilderness of the far north—Oh, little baby, let us raise our cups together, yours with milk and mine with wine, and in milk and wine drink together to that wise, good, charitable providence that wrecked us—*Here!*»

«And, oh Danes, may God bless you!»

Then, draining my glass, I sat quickly down for I was beginning to talk too much.

And from then on, sadly, more and more, I thought:

«Tomorrow I sail; tomorrow I sail.»

And at that party were:

Direktör Daugaard-Jensen, Landsfoged Knud Oldendov og Frue, Kolonibestyrer Simony og Frue, Kolonibestyrer Ibsen og Frue, Provst Vestergaard og Frue, Kredslæge P. Borresen, Frk. Holmgaard, Læge Hr. Holbeck, Læge Frk. Gudrun Christiansen, Læge Hr. Christensen, Ingeniör Niels Jagd, Ingeniör Galster,

Seminarieforstander N. E. Balle og Frue, Seminarielærer A. Bjerge og Frue, Radiotelegrafist Wodschow, Assistent Leif Hagensen og Frue, Rævestutteribestyrer Högle og Frue, Assistent Lund og Frue.

Kaptajn Hansen, Kaptajn Thorsen, Kaptajn Bang, Hr. Erik Valeur, Frk. Munch, Kaptajn Herschend.

Dr. Phil. Knud Rasmussen, Frk. Inge Rasmussen, Hr. Peter Freuchen og Frue, Hr. Porsild, Professor Nörlund, Forfatter Axel Ahlman.

THE morrow dawned—most fair to add most poignancy to parting. And although the sun rose, to be sure, over the mountains I was less steadfast to my memories of sunrise than the wanderer of Aluk; I grieved at going. But many grieved that day.

Tina, a little Greenland girl who since leaving the north had at each stopping place left more and more of all her store of clothes as presents to whoever liked her, now leaves her kindred and stands red-eyed, weeping at the rail.

A doctor is departing from Greenland, maybe forever. Natives in kayaks hover near the ship. They fire volleys from their shot guns as she gathers speed, and follow, waving caps. There stands the doctor, monument of calm. I move to join him, and stop short. He's crying.

So—many weep. And if the depth and sweetness of the human soul may be appraised by its responsiveness to sorrow here at the steamer's rail see Danes and Eskimos alike moved in a common crisis to a common grief. It was the wilderness that bore and nurtured and determined man; not the millenniums nor the mutations of his culture, not law nor custom nor belief nor circumstance, not any power in ten thousand centuries has changed or can man's imminence.

«Farvel!» The cloud-wreathed cape is passed. Greenland is memory like all the rest. The wide circle of the ocean's horizon is around me, a huge zero, the symbol of my momentary nowhere. Like Orulo, an Eskimo of Cape Elizabeth, I've told my story; let me like Orulo end it. For a long time Knud Rasmussen had sat entranced, listening to her story. She paused:

«And that,» she said, «is the end of my adventures. For one who lives happily has no adventures, and in truth I have lived happily and have had seven children.»

APPENDIX

APPENDIX

APPENDIX

THE Eskimo poems that follow are presented first for their naïve charm and frequent loveliness; then that whoever feels their loveliness and charm may feel and know the kinship of his soul with those of stone-age men. Of the unchangeableness of man's profounder nature that kinship *felt* may be the strongest evidence.

The poems, or songs as they more truly are, stem from pre-European days; they are traditional and form a part of the inherited culture of the Eskimos and Greenlanders of today. They have been translated twice to here emerge in English. But inasmuch as scientists have been their sponsors we may suspect whatever beauty their present form allows them to have been robustly inherent to the imagery of the originals.

The first six poems are from an article by C. W. Schultz-Lorentzen in *Greenland*, Vol. II, published by the commission for the Direction of Geological and Geographical Investigations in Greenland. The first and fourth poems were transcribed from the Eskimo by W. Thalbitzer; the second, third, fifth and sixth by Knud Rasmussen. Numbers seven to thirteen are from *Across Arctic America* and the fourteenth from the *Report of the Fifth Thule Expedition 1921–24*, both by Knud Rasmussen.

The black-bluish spot referred to in the first poem appears on Eskimo children, as on the children of the Japanese and other East-Asiatic peoples; it is generally below the small of the back.

It was the ancient custom among Greenlanders, before the majesty of European law invaded their lives, to resolve their quarrels by a contest of song. Of that custom Hans Egede has written:

«They show their wit chiefly in satirical songs, which they compose against one another; and he, that overcomes his fellow in this way of debate, is admired and applauded by the rest of the assembly. If anybody conceives a jealousy, or bears a grudge to another upon any account, he sends to him, and challenges him to a duel in such or such assembly; where he will fight it out with him in taunting ditties. Whereupon the defied, in defence of his honour, prepares his weapons, and does not fail to appear at the time and place appointed, if his courage do not forsake him. When the assembly is met, and the combatants arrived, everybody being silent and attentive to hear what end the combat will take, the challenger first enters the lists, and begins to sing, accompanying it with the beat of his drum. The challenged rises also, and in silence listens, until his champion or adversary has done singing. Then he likewise enters the lists, armed with the same weapons, and lays about his party the best he can. And thus they alternately sing as long as their stock of ditties lasts. He that first gives over is reckoned overcome and conquered. In this sort of taunting ditties they reproach and upbraid one another with their failings. And this is their common way of taking vengeance.»

Number six is a «taunting ditty.»

The picture-making of the primitive Eskimos is of the character to furnish biologists with evidence for their conclusion that the mind of the primitive is similar to that of the child. It isn't. A culture is not a measure for the potentialities of men; it has its own organic, independent growth. And those pictures herewith reproduced, having been made by Greenlanders under the influence of European art and with the tools and materials of the craft of wood cutting, resemble and are fully comparable to the more ordinary works of the wood cut period in European graphic art.

Figure 1 is taken from Nansen's *In Northern Mists*, Figure 2 from the periodical *Atuagagdliutit*, edited, printed and published by Greenlanders. The other pictures are from the book *Kaladlit Assilialiait*, printed by the Greenlander Lars Möller, Godthaab, 1860.

I

Little whimpering babe,
little suckling babe
nestle against mother.
How she burns, how she burns,
straddling, she makes warm
my arm and my hands.
Down there is the black-bluish spot
which will never come off
however much I lick
her tender little loins.
How she whimpers, how she begs
little troublesome girl of mine.

II

A small ptarmigan sat
on the beautiful plain
perched on a drift of snow.
Red were its eyelids
brown was it down its back
and between its small posteriors
was the dearest little anus.

III

Aja-ha, aja-ha
I was out in a kayak
and went ashore,
aja-ha, aja-ha;
here I found a drift of snow,
and it had begun to melt.
Aja-hai-ja, aja-hai-ja.
Then I knew it was spring
and that we had lived through the winter.
Aja-hai-ja, aja-ha.
And I was so afraid that my eyes
should be far too weak,
far too weak
to see all the beautiful things.
Aja-hai-ja,
aja-hai-ja,
ajaiha.

IV

So deep a sorrow came upon me!
Sorrow settles heavily upon my mind
while I am gathering berries on the mountain,
so deep a sorrow is coming upon me.
My sun rises quickly upon it,
sorrow settles heavily on my mind.
How the sea down there, right off our village
lies quietly and at rest.
The dear, great kayak men
are going out on it.
Sorrow settled heavily upon me,
while I gathered berries on the mountain.

V

Ijaja—ijaja, aje,
Let me try to get my thought
my great thought,
at some distance,
ijaja—ijaja-aje.

Let me try to swallow,
to get away from the throat
my great sorrow.
ijaja-a—ijaja-aje.

Let my song
carry it some distance away from me
let my song
breathe it away from my throat,
let my clumsy little song
lift my great sorrow
out of my mind.
ija-ja—ijaja-aje.

But no, no, no,
it is impossible
to tear my pain from my throat,
it is impossible
to let loose the weeping which presses.
ijaja-a—ijaja-aje.

My eyes are tired
my worn-out eyes
which never more will follow the narwhal
when shooting up from the deep
in order to break the waves of the sea,
and my muscles will nevermore tremble
when I seize the harpoon.
ijaja-a—ijaja-aje.

Wish that the souls
of the great sea animals I killed
would help me to get
my heavy thoughts to a distance.
Wish that the memory
of all my great hunts
might lift me out of
the weakness of old age.
ijaja-a—ijaja-aje.

Let my breath blow a song
of the animals I have caught,
of the narwhals
when the shoals broke the surface of the sea
in foaming breakers off my village.
Aputiteq
ijaja-a—ijaja-aje.

The throaty songs of the narwhals
sounded through their blowing
when they spouted
some in deep tones, others in shrill whistling.
The narwhals which rested
sleepy and dozing, flock by flock
on the surface of the sea.
Of all this which calls to mind
my youth
I am singing.
And my song breaks from my throat
with the breath of my life.

VI

Assailant: Let me split words,
       small, sharp words
       like wood I split
       with an axe.
       A song from old times
       A breath from my forefathers
       A Lethean song for my wife
       A song which may sink the longing
       overpowering me.
       A bold chatterer has taken her away,
       has tried to make her less,
       a miserable who loves human flesh
       a cannibal from time of starvation.

Adversary: Boldness that surprises!
       Mock anger and courage!
       A libellous ditty
       throwing the blame on me!
       Fear thou wilt strike into me
       while careless I expose myself to be killed.
       Hie—thou singest about my wife
       who once was thine;
       then thou wert not nearly so lovable.

While she was alone
Thou forgottest to praise her in song,
in challenging battle songs.
Now she is mine,
nor shall she visit false lovers,
beautifully singing lovers of women
in strange tents.

VII

I am but a little woman
very willing to toil,
very willing and happy
to work and slave . . . .
And in my eagerness
to be of use,
I pluck the furry buds of willow
buds like beard of wolf.

I love to go walking far and far away,
and my soles are worn through
as I pluck the buds of willow,
that are furry like the great wolf's beard. . . .

VIII

I draw a deep breath,
but my breath comes heavily
as I call forth the song. . . .

There are ill rumors abroad,
of some who starve in the far places,
and can find no meat.

I call forth the song
from above,
Hayaya—haya.

And now I forget
how hard it was to breathe,
remembering old times,
when I had strength
to cut and flay great beasts.
Three great beasts could I cut up
while the sun slowly went his way
across the sky.

IX

Only the Air-spirits know
what lies beyond the hills,
yet I urge my team farther on,
drive on and on,
on and on!

X

O father- and motherless,
O dear little one-all-alone
give me
boots of caribou.
Bring me a gift,
a beast of those beasts
that make luscious blood soup;
a beast of the beasts
from the depths of the sea
and not from the plains of earth.
Little father- and motherless one,
bring me a gift.

XI

I will sing a song,
a little song about myself
I have lain sick since the autumn
and now I am weak as a child,
Unaya—unaya.

Sad at heart I wish
my woman away in the house of another
in the house of a man
who may be her refuge,
firm and sure as the strong winter ice.

Sad at heart I wish her away
in the house of a stronger protector
now that I myself lack strength
even to rise from where I lie.
Unaya—unaya.

Who knoweth his fate?
Here I lie, weak and unable to rise,
and only my memories are strong.

XII

I will visit
unknown woman,
search out hidden things
behind the man.
   Let the boot-thong hang loose—
seek thou under man
and under woman!
Smooth out the wrinkled cheeks,
smooth wrinkles out.

I walked on the ice of the sea,
   Seal were blowing at the blowholes—
wondering I heard
the song of the sea
and the great sighing of the new formed ice.
Go, then, go!
Strength of soul brings health
to the place of feasting.

XIII

There is fear
in the longing for loneliness
when gathered with friends,
and, longing to be alone.
Iyaiya-yaya!

There is joy
in feeling the summer
come to the great world,
and watching the sun
follow its ancient way.
Iyaiya-yaya!

There is fear
in feeling the winter
come to the great world
and watching the moon
now half-moon, now full,
follow its ancient way.
Iyaiya-yaya!

Whither is all this tending?
I would I were far to the eastward.
And yet I shall never again
Meet with my kinsman.
Iyaiya-yaya!

XIV

Ajaja-aja-ja ja,
The lands around my dwelling
are more beautiful
from the day
when it is given me to see
faces I have never seen before.
All is more beautiful,
all is more beautiful,
and life is thankfulness.
These guests of mine
make my house grand,
Ajaja-aja-ja ja.

DESIGNED BY ROCKWELL KENT THIS TRADE
EDITION OF N BY E WAS PRINTED IN 1930
AT THE LAKESIDE PRESS, CHICAGO, UNDER
THE SUPERVISION OF WILLIAM A. KITTREDGE